What an inspiration, both this book and its author. If anyone knows how to build for success, it is LeRoy Bailey. He's been there, he's done that. This book is a winner for winners. Read it!

—Dr. Robert Schuller
New York Times Best-selling Author
Senior Pastor of The Crystal Cathedral,
Garden Grove, CA

Here is a delightful and insightful book, written by one of the most outstanding leaders of our time, LeRoy Bailey, who knows how to build solidly from the ground up, whether in the life of God's church or in one's personal life. Anyone who reads this book will be powerfully inspired and blessed.

—Donald W. Morgan
Author of *When Your World Is Coming Apart*
and *Share the Dream, Build the Team*

"Profoundly simple and simply profound" best describes this book of blessings. Bishop Bailey keeps it real by reminding us that when it comes to great things in God, there is no express elevator to the top. This is a much-needed word in a culture that has a microwave mentality. This is not just a thesis but a testimony of how God can turn little into much if you start with a solid foundation.

—Bishop Tom Garrott Benjamin Jr., D. Min.
Light of the World Christian Church
Indianapolis, IN

Albert Einstein shared that, "The only reason for time is so that everything doesn't happen at once." This quote came to mind immediately when I began reading this wonderful, anointed book by Dr. LeRoy Bailey. I only wish there was a way to make this book mandatory for all of our Christian high school and college students.

All of us have experienced mistakes, loss, and grief, many times because we fail to implement the principle that Dr. Bailey so expertly reveals in this book: Success is determined by our willingness to count the cost and then invest in laying a solid foundation.

Dr. Bailey's advice, wrapped around the story of his own life, provides great insight on patience, health, rest, financial savvy, and wise counsel. It encourages readers to regroup, rebuild, and reestablish their lives, finances, ministries, professions, and relationships.

Thank you, Dr. Bailey, for telling it like it is. Your truthful, honest, and passionate examples have blessed my life, time and time again. Thank you for giving us permission to take off our masks and deal honestly with who we are and what our God-given destiny really is.

—Dr. Wanda A. Turner
Christian Author, Speaker, and Businesswoman

# A SOLID FOUNDATION

## DR. LEROY BAILEY

## A SOLID FOUNDATION

Dr. LeRoy Bailey
The First Cathedral
1151 Blue Hills Avenue
Bloomfield, CT 06002

ISBN: 0-88368-777-1
Printed in the United States of America
© 2003 by Dr. LeRoy Bailey Jr.

Whitaker House
30 Hunt Valley Circle
New Kensington, PA 15068
website: www.whitakerhouse.com

Library of Congress Cataloging-in-Publication Data

Bailey, LeRoy, 1946–
 A solid foundation : building your life from the ground up / by LeRoy
Bailey.
     p. cm.
 ISBN 0-88368-777-1 (pbk. : alk. paper)
 1. Christian life. I. Title.
 BV4501.3.B34 2003
 248.4—dc21
                    2003008911

1 2 3 4 5 6 7 8 9 10 11 12 13 / 10 09 08 07 06 05 04 03

# Dedication

---

This book is dedicated to my wife, Mrs. Reathie Bailey, and my three children, LeRoy, Riva, and Michael.

# Acknowledgements

It is a difficult task to thank every single person that has positively affected me throughout the course of my life. However, I will attempt to mention just of few of those whom I can recall most easily. First, I would like to acknowledge my father in the ministry and his wife, the late Rev. and Mrs. L. A. Hamblin, who are responsible for much of the solid foundation upon which I have built great things for the Lord. Special thanks to my father, the late Lee Bailey. A very special thanks goes to my mother, Verneda E. Breathett, whose loving support continues to be a wellspring of much-needed encouragement. I would also like to acknowledge my two siblings, Greta Owens and Yvonne Marie Holt, for their loving support over the years.

I would like to thank The First Cathedral family, whom I have had the great fortune of shepherding for the past thirty-two years. They have supplied me with resources and opened their hearts to me, allowing me to fully utilize my strengths and giftings for the sake of the kingdom. I thank them most for allowing me to grow in Christ, side by side with them.

Thanks Mary Bragg, my executive administrator, for her clerical assistance on this project.

Special thanks to my spiritual son, Pastor Aaron D. Lewis, for his inspiration and his assistance in the development of this project.

I would like to thank all of my spiritual sons and daughters across the nation and around the world. It is my greatest desire that you will fulfill your spiritual vision wherever God leads you.

As is customary, I have saved the very best for last. I would like to thank my three children, Riva, LeRoy III, and Michael, for unselfishly sharing their father with the world so that many would know Jesus. To my wife, Mrs. Reathie Bailey, who is truly the irreplaceable love of my life; you are the natural driving force behind all of my achievements. And finally, I thank the Lord Jesus Christ, who is my Savior, my truest Love, and my personal Friend. It is He alone who has given me the ability to do great works for Him.

# Contents

# Introduction

I t was a pleasant and unexpected surprise to pick up our local newspaper one Sunday in 1999 and read a very favorable review of some of the recent events surrounding the dedication of our new sanctuary. It read:

## A Preacher's Vision Made Real

The applause began as the Rev. LeRoy Bailey Jr. rose from his chair on the altar of First Cathedral, and it grew in intensity and filled the cavernous sanctuary as he slowly walked to the podium. By the time Bailey finished his short journey and stood before his congregation for the first time in its new home, more than 2,500 people were on their feet in recognition of the much longer journey he had led them on. It was Bailey's vision, they said Saturday, that guided the First Baptist Church of Hartford from its inception as a group of 60 people meeting in homes in 1968 to a 7,000-member congregation that built the $13 million cathedral they dedicated Saturday.

—*The Hartford Courant*
Sunday, September 5, 1999

Despite the many accolades, gifts, and well-wishing remarks I received throughout that dedicatory weekend, I knew better than anyone else to whom all the credit was really due. Had it not been for the prevailing presence of the Holy Spirit in my life, in our church, and in our church's activities, this dream would never have become reality. God had taken a young African-American man from the South and given him this wonderful success. We had secured the best architects, engineers, and builders our money could buy for our new facility, but long before the work was physically completed, it had already been completed in the mind of the Chief Architect—the Lord Jesus Christ Himself. Without His guidance and direction, none of what I beheld that day would have existed.

The disciple John wrote, *"All things were made through Him, and without Him nothing was made that was made"* (John 1:3). While this verse refers to God's Creation of the world, I now see that its truth applies to our lives today, as well. All things that come to pass do so because He sustains His creation and brings His perfect will to fruition.

God had been so good to me during the expansion of our church, and His working through me surpassed all that I could possibly have dreamed. I did not possess the skills to physically erect such a grand cathedral, for I was neither a builder nor an engineer. If there was anything I *could* claim to be, it was a preacher of righteousness, and that was wholly a gift from God, as well, not anything of my own doing. Yet everyone was now asking me to reveal the secret of our church's success.

It was not a new question. As I had traveled throughout America, many had approached me and asked the same question. I could understand their curiosity. Several thousand people attended our church each week, and we were building our modern cathedral with seating for 3,400. We had our own elementary school and even a school of ministry. We also had a close working relationship with Churches Uniting in Global Missions (CUGM) because of the heart God had given us for foreign and domestic missions. People were curious to know how we had accomplished it all.

"How did your church grow so large so fast?" I was asked. "What one thing did you do to make things happen?" "How can I duplicate your success?" "What's your secret?" My answer to everyone who asked was always the same: *a solid foundation.* Not surprisingly, this short answer seemed totally inadequate for some and even evasive to others. In all sincerity, though, I could not think of any other single element that would best explain the truth behind what God had done in the life of our church. He had led us to lay a solid foundation before undertaking any tasks, and it was this foundation in our ministry—carefully, thoughtfully, and painstakingly constructed—that permitted the success God was now allowing our church to enjoy.

Even as I gave my short answer, I realized that most of those who asked me these questions were expecting something more. Modern Americans are constantly searching for the revelation of some secret formula that might cause their ministries, businesses, or careers to automatically change for the better overnight. A glance at the top headlines in today's magazines or at the titles in our bookstores' "self-improvement" sections attest to this truth. Promises such as "Financial Success in 10 Easy Steps!" or "Debt-Free in Days!" are not uncommon. But the truth of the matter is that I didn't know any such secret or easy-to-follow plan. I still don't. After more than forty-five years of ministry and service, I have come to believe that formulas for quick and easy success simply don't exist. Building on a solid foundation is the only magic formula I know.

Unfortunately, many people are not too happy when they hear an answer like that. We live in a high-speed culture and are plagued by what I like to call the "fast-food mentality." This way of thinking has caused us to become childishly impatient and eager to embrace quick fixes in theology that, all too often, discount the importance of long processes that are necessary in the development of our spiritual maturity. Worst of all, the fast-food mentality has given us the false notion that great things can be established overnight. As a result, instead of embracing God-given opportunities to build something of lasting worth, we often decline because we are so eager to achieve noble status quickly. We've become unwilling to invest the time and effort necessary for long-term results.

What so many fail to realize is that success is found in those who have a track record—which may indeed include many failures. It is our tests that validate our testimonies. Before God can produce anything great in us, we first must be tested over time. Although themes like developing patience, awaiting God's timing, and enduring trials are far from popular these days, they are essential lessons we must learn if we hope to develop the character needed to complete tasks worthy of God's approval.

Joseph learned these lessons, as the Old Testament records: *"He sent a man before them; Joseph; who was sold as a slave. They hurt his feet with fetters, he was laid in irons. Until the time that his word came to pass, the word of the LORD tested him"* (Psalm 105:17–19). The success that Joseph tasted as Pharaoh's secondhand man didn't come quickly or easily. It took time—and a great deal of suffering in Joseph's case—before *"his word came to pass."* As a popular Christian band explains it in one of their songs, we have to experience the *means* before we reach the *ends*. Results come only after we've undergone the process.

There are some things in life that will only happen with time. They can't be hurried through, just as a loaf of bread can't be rushed. Time is an essential ingredient in the making of bread, and ignoring the time that bread needs to rise and bake would be as foolish as ignoring the recipe's call for flour. Bread will not be bread, but rather a big cracker, if we deprive it of the time required for the yeast to do its work. And bread will not be bread, but rather a big ball of dough, if we neglect to give it enough time in the oven. Similarly, the outcomes in our lives will not be what they should unless we give them the time they need to come to completion.

It has often been said that Rome wasn't built in a day, and I'm of the opinion that this saying should be revisited often as we remind ourselves that anything of lasting value requires time to build. That's what this book is all about. Whether you are trying to build a business, a ministry, a marriage relationship, a friendship, or your financial future, it must have a solid foundation, one that will stand the test of time. I cannot guarantee you overnight success or quick fixes. I can, however, place within your hands a few essential elements that you can use to start building toward the fulfillment of your God-given dream.

—Dr. LeRoy Bailey
Senior Pastor of The First Cathedral
Hartford, CT

# Part I

# The Far-Reaching Effects of Foundations

# Chapter One
# Is It Worth the Time?

*Therefore whoever hears these sayings of Mine, and does*
*them, I will liken him to a wise man who built his house*
*on the rock: and the rain descended, the floods came, and*
*the winds blew and beat on that house; and it did not fall,*
*for it was founded on the rock. But everyone who hears*
*these sayings of Mine, and does not do them, will be like a*
*foolish man who built his house on the sand: and the rain*
*descended, the floods came, and the winds blew and beat*
*on that house; and it fell. And great was its fall.*
—Matthew 7:24–27

Many years ago in downtown Hartford, I noticed that work had begun on a building that would eventually house Channel 61 Television. The building would become one of Hartford's tallest and most remarkable structures, but as I had occasion to pass by that construction site over the ensuing months, I noticed something strange: The building was very slow to rise above the level of the construction fence. For more than a year, in fact, not a single wall was erected, not a single window was installed, and no roofing system was put into place. The aboveground construction had not yet even begun, and all that time, workday after workday, the contractors were investing their efforts into one single element of the building—the foundation. That amazed me. More than a year's worth of time and energy (not to mention steel and concrete) were invested into the foundation of a single structure—and all of that was underground, where no one would ever see it. What importance these builders placed on their foundation!

When the aboveground structure finally did begin to rise, it went up rather quickly. Proportionately speaking, more time had been invested into the foundation than into any other part of the building. The foundation was the key element of the building, and its strength and integrity would determine just how high the building could stand.

Think about that! *The time spent laying the foundation of that building determined how high the building could reach.* If very little time had been spent preparing the foundation, the building might have been limited to only two or three stories. But in order for the building to stand tall and strong and to last through many years, its foundation had to be well thought-out, well designed, and skillfully constructed. What patience those workers had to employ! Without patience, nothing of lasting worth is ever produced.

> Without patience, nothing of lasting worth is ever produced.

Whatever you decide to build in life, make sure that you invest more time in preparing its foundation than in any other part. Also, be sure to ask God to give you the patience that must accompany any such feat. James, who called himself *"a bondservant of God and of the Lord Jesus Christ"* (James 1:1), confirmed what I'm saying in the book of the

Bible bearing his name. His words concerning faith and patience must become our guiding light as we look at our long-term, God-inspired dreams and goals and realize how to reach them:

> *My brethren, count it all joy when you fall into various trials, knowing that the testing of your faith produces patience. But let patience have its perfect work, that you may be perfect and complete, lacking nothing. If any of you lacks wisdom, let him ask of God, who gives to all liberally and without reproach, and it will be given to him. But let him ask in faith, with no doubting, for he who doubts is like a wave of the sea driven and tossed by the wind. For let not that man suppose that he will receive anything from the Lord; he is a double-minded man, unstable in all his ways.* (James 1:2–8)

Because we live in a society where quick fixes and high-speed results are expected, we require proof, some convincing evidence, that investing our time into building a solid foundation will be rewarded. After all, why would any of us want to sow precious time into something that may turn out to be an empty promise?

Within every society, there are highly visible personalities who are applauded and celebrated for their high achievements. These high achievements might be in the arts, in science, in education, in business, in sports, in spiritual leadership, or in social activism. Whatever the particular vocation might be, each of these outstanding personalities has needed a solid foundation upon which to build success. While many may have the appearance of success, those who enjoy true success and greatness that passes the test of time are those who have laid solid foundations and have built the necessary infrastructures.

Successes are made over a lifetime, not overnight, and to ignore the need for a solid foundation would be to ignore the element that will eventually bear the great weight of each success. A house without a foundation will fall, as will anything without proper grounding. Laying a good foundation, although it may take time, will provide you with a strong platform on which to firmly stand when your time for success arrives.

## The Benefit of Using Financial Examples

Using examples that center around money have proven, for me, to be a particularly useful way of getting my points across as a pastor. Although there are other examples that I could use, the importance of money in our lives seems to appropriately convey the urgent need for a solid foundation. To my way of thinking, this style of instruction makes difficult concepts easier to understand, and most people listen when we talk money.

The average person would like to have more money. Some hide behind a religious mask and deny this, but it's true nonetheless. What is the main reason that employees put in overtime hours, ask for raises, and demand promotions at their jobs? It's clear that they want (or need) more money. Most people don't work extra hours without expecting some compensation in return. Unfortunately, many people are still financially unsatisfied, even after they get raises and promotions. This, I believe, is because many people have ignored the basic fundamentals about money—fundamentals that must be grasped if one is to prosper financially.

Ignorance concerning the need for a solid foundation is the reason why nearly one-third of lottery winners go broke—not only financially, but also emotionally, physically, and mentally. [1] How is it possible that a person can win so much money and, within a few years, be once more in financial need? It is clear that a proper foundation is missing in cases such as this.

A person who understands the laws that govern wealth—including basic accounting principles and investment strategies—will not merely keep the money he currently has but will also take steps to make that money multiply many times over. This principle is the foundation for financial increase, and the person who ignores it is surely headed for financial disaster. Without investment there is no return.

> Without investment there is no return.

This governing law of wealth has its counterpart in the spiritual realm. The apostle Paul wrote to the Galatian believers: *"Do not be deceived, God is not mocked; for whatever a man sows, that he will also reap"* (Galatians 6:7). This principle expresses a very basic theme that is foundational to many spiritual laws. No matter what you expect to harvest, you will reap only what you have sown. If you sow much, you will reap much. For example, if you sow time into building godly relationships with those around you, you can expect to reap fulfilling, God-honoring relationships. If you spend very little time investing in such relationships, however, you can't expect to reap them. Similarly, in the financial realm, the believer who has difficulty sowing his finances into the kingdom of God may experience difficulty in receiving. This helps explain why some people work two, three, or even four jobs just to make ends meet, never getting ahead because they choose to ignore the basic principles governing prosperity.

---

1. Paul Tharp, "Lottery Raises Issues of Cents and Sensibilities," *New York Post* (November 14, 1997). <http://www.family.org/cforum/hotissues/A0001276.html> (16 April, 2003)

You see, hard work does not guarantee that a person can live the kind of lifestyle he or she would like to. Understanding and implementing biblically-based spiritual laws, however, allows a person to exhibit sound financial wisdom, which often results in a very rewarding lifestyle. I have seen people in my own congregation work themselves nearly to death in their efforts to achieve a certain lifestyle, and yet remain broke. On the other hand, I have seen single women in my church work only one job (and one that didn't pay very well) and yet always have their needs met, largely because they are faithful in paying their tithes and bringing their offerings to God. While it's not an iron-clad promise that obedience results in an easy, stress-free life, people who are faithful in sowing as the Lord has called them to often possess a great sense of peace and comfort.

People who get money easily usually don't respect it. They have no concept of why money comes to some and not to others. Because it came easily to them at one time, they expect it to always come that way. When the tides change and the money stops coming so easily, they're not prepared and are left baffled, scratching their heads, trying to figure out what went wrong. Money flees the person who does not respect it or take time to figure out how it works. Those who take time to learn about it thus build a solid financial foundation and are more likely to have the money they need.

Those who care about having a strong financial future are not afraid to read books that deal with business and money. They often read periodicals such as *Money, Worth, Success, Forbes,* or *Fortune.* They read the business and money sections of their local newspapers and frequently refer to *The Wall Street Journal* for up-to-date information concerning the movement of stocks and bonds, thus making themselves as aware as possible of ever-changing trends in the marketplace. Often they will even attend seminars that teach basic principles about finances and financial management. Ultimately, they look to God's Word as the supreme resource and reference book—not just for their finances but rather for all realms of their lives. They prayerfully seek after God's guidance to secure wealth in a righteous manner that is pleasing to Him. Such diligence creates a solid foundation that can support a healthy financial future. On the other hand, disregarding financial wisdom paves the way for life-long poverty.

# The Double-Dealing Accountant of the Bible

One of the saddest stories in the entire Bible substantiates my point. In one of Jesus' parables, an unjust steward was commended for the wisdom he used after he had, quite literally, defrauded his masters out of their money. In the same text, Jesus revealed why the children of this world have a potential advantage over the children of righteousness when it comes to the financial arena. Clearly, there is much that we can learn from this narrative.

The story goes something like this: A rich man hired a personal accountant to help him keep his financial books in order. One day, the rich man discovered that his accountant had been stealing money from his accounts. The employer confronted the man about the matter and decided to fire him. Because he was a white-collar worker, the accountant knew nothing about manual labor. If he could not think of an alternative plan of action quickly, he would soon be out of work and possibly homeless and starving.

It was then that a thought came to him. He would "cut a deal" with all who owed his employer money. He discounted each of the debtors' bills by 20 to 50 percent in an attempt to secure their goodwill and help for when he became unemployed. These debtors, of course, were very grateful to the accountant for this favor. When his employer discovered what had been done, although it was thoroughly dishonest, he actually commended the accountant for his shrewdness in doing business. Through his financial savvy, he had ensured that he would always have a place to work. He understood how to use money to influence people, and he used that knowledge to guarantee that he would have employment in the future.

> *So the master commended the unjust steward because he had dealt shrewdly. For the sons of this world are more shrewd in their generation than the sons of light. And I say to you, make friends for yourselves by unrighteous mammon, that when you fail, they may receive you into an everlasting home. He who is faithful in what is least is faithful also in much; and he who is unjust in what is least is unjust also in much.* (Luke 16:8–10)

Some have interpreted this parable as a godly mandate against wealth, avarice, and the possession of material things. Others have read into it an explanation of the dangers of dishonesty and how cheating may bar some from entering into the kingdom of God. Although greed is obviously not a spiritual virtue and dishonest transactions are not a part of godly living, I believe that this Scripture is trying to communicate a foundational truth that many may miss.

First, when the master praised the dishonest man, he was certainly not praising him for being a thief. In his part of the world, thieves were severely punished. So the man must have been commended for something very different.

Jesus says that the master's praises were because the steward *"had done wisely."* These congratulations were not for dishonesty but rather for the worldly wisdom the steward used. This lesson, the call to wise Christian action, is one that many children of Light have yet to learn. Just as the steward used wisdom to achieve his worldly ends, so too do we as Christians need to exercise wisdom in attaining the ends to which God has called us.

The person who continually ignores periodicals, magazines, and books that deal with the topic of money, for instance, will be more likely to have money taken from him. This same type of person will always be drawn to "get-rich-quick" schemes and opportunities that appear "too good to be true" (and probably are). A person who chooses the way of wisdom, however, will taste rewards.

Another parable about the proper use of money, the parable of the talents, tells the story of three men. One of them had no desire to learn about investing. His two counterparts invested the little money they had been given, choosing to utilize their foundational knowledge of finances, and both reaped a one-hundred-percent return on their investments. The first man, the one who decided to make excuses rather than take any action, buried his money. Because he had no basic knowledge of finance and the principles governing it, he did not understand or care about the various options that were at his fingertips, and so he acted unwisely.

He could have invested the money. If, like many, he had no desire to involve himself in the risks of investing, he could have put the money into some type of savings account to draw interest. Another option would have been to trade his money for something of greater value. He could have sown his money into some good cause and reaped God's blessing on his life as a result. Instead, he chose to do nothing. As a result, his lord said of him:

> *Therefore take the talent from him, and give it to him who has ten talents. For to everyone who has,*

*more will be given, and he will have abundance; but from him who does not have, even what he has will be taken away. And cast the unprofitable servant into the outer darkness. There will be weeping and gnashing of teeth.* (Matthew 25:28–30)

Unfortunately, this man's actions cost him much more than the funds he failed to appreciate and use wisely. The very funds he tried to protect by not investing were ultimately lost, for his master took them away and gave them to the man who had the most. In some ways, this mirrors the sad truth that the rich get richer, and the poor get poorer, but, in this case, the reason the rich get richer is clear and simple: They study and put into practice the principles governing money. The poor, on the other hand, often know more about debt than they do about saving and investing. Since they do not take time to understand the principles of saving and investing, they never practice them and thus end up deeper in debt.

The fundamental message in all this is that the more you learn about finances, the more opportunity you will have for increase. The better you lay a solid foundation in your financial dealings, the more chances you will have for success. Experiencing financial success requires having a strong financial foundation. You need to lay the foundation, however long it may take, before you can build your skyscraper.

In this first chapter, we've carefully examined how a strong financial foundation is essential to a healthy financial return. And, as I said at the start of this chapter, finances are just an example. The principle of a solid foundation applies to *all* areas of life, whether they are financial, physical, familial, emotional, or spiritual. When you take the time to *invest,* as the two wise stewards did, and make the effort to *act wisely,* as the shrewd servant did, you can expect an abundant return.

So, returning to the title of this chapter, is it worth the time to lay a solid foundation? Most certainly. To build upon sinking sand—or, worse yet, to build upon no foundation at all—is the real time-waster, for anything not built upon a solid foundation will crumble and collapse in the end.

*Therefore whoever hears these sayings of Mine, and does them, I will liken him to a wise man who built his house on the rock: and the rain descended, the floods came, and the winds blew and beat on that house; and it did not fall, for it was founded on the rock. But everyone who hears these sayings of Mine, and does not do them, will be like a foolish man who built his house on the sand: and the rain descended, the floods came, and the winds blew and beat on that house; and it fell. And great was its fall.* (Matthew 7:24–27)

# Chapter Two
# The Cornerstone for a Solid Foundation

J ust as a solid foundation is fundamental to the stability of the structure built upon it, so too is the cornerstone crucial to the solidity of the foundation. Without a cornerstone, the foundation itself is not stable or strong. The cornerstone is essential.

What is a cornerstone? Perhaps you've heard the term used as a synonym for *foundation*. Someone might say, "The cornerstone of this company is..." or "The cornerstone of this ministry is...," referring to the principles on which the company or the ministry was built. However, structurally speaking, the cornerstone is not synonymous to the foundation but rather a special and unique part of the foundation. It is laid even before the long process of laying the foundation begins.

*The American Heritage Dictionary* defines *cornerstone* as "A stone at the corner of a building uniting two intersecting walls." [1] *Vine's Expository Dictionary of New Testament Words* provides even more insight into the importance of cornerstones: "They were laid so as to give strength to the two walls with which they were connected." [2] In other words, the very strength of the building itself depends on the cornerstone. At the cornerstone, the whole structure is united, strengthened, and held together. It is the "foundation," so to speak, of the foundation itself.

> Our cornerstones are found in vision.

Clearly, we need cornerstones before we can start building our foundations. Where do we get these cornerstones to start building the foundations of our lives upon? As the story of the apostle Paul teaches us, our cornerstones are found in vision.

## Paul's Story: The Value of Vision

Late in his life, Paul found himself having to explain and defend his ministry to the "higher-ups" in the Roman government because of accusations brought against him by the Jews. In a defense addressed to King Agrippa, Paul began by describing the foundation he *once* built his life upon, when he was still called Saul, before he met the Lord Jesus Christ on the road to Damascus.

*My manner of life from my youth, which was spent from the beginning among my own nation at Jerusalem, all the Jews know. They knew me from the first, if they were willing to testify, that*

1. *The American Heritage® Dictionary of the English Language,* 4th ed., s.v. "cornerstone."
2. *Vine's Expository Dictionary of New Testament Words: A Comprehensive Dictionary of the Original Greek Words with Their Precise Meanings for English Readers,* Unabridged Edition (MacDonald Publishing Company), s.v. "corner, cornerstone."

*according to the strictest sect of our religion I lived a Pharisee....Indeed, I myself thought I must do many things contrary to the name of Jesus of Nazareth. This I also did in Jerusalem, and many of the saints I shut up in prison, having received authority from the chief priests; and when they were put to death, I cast my vote against them. And I punished them often in every synagogue and compelled them to blaspheme; and being exceedingly enraged against them, I persecuted them even to foreign cities.*

(Acts 26:4–5; 9–11)

Paul's pre-Christian foundation was extreme adherence to the law, even to the point of persecuting those who no longer adhered to that law. When his name changed from Saul to Paul, however, his foundation changed as well.

*While thus occupied, as I journeyed to Damascus with authority and commission from the chief priests, at midday, O king, along the road I saw a light from heaven, brighter than the sun, shining around me and those who journeyed with me. And when we all had fallen to the ground, I heard a voice speaking to me and saying in the Hebrew language, "Saul, Saul, why are you persecuting Me? It is hard for you to kick against the goads." So I said, "Who are You, Lord?" And He said, "I am Jesus, whom you are persecuting. But rise and stand on your feet; for I have appeared to you for this purpose, to make you a minister and a witness both of the things which you have seen and of the things which I will yet reveal to you. I will deliver you from the Jewish people, as well as from the Gentiles, to whom I now send you, to open their eyes, in order to turn them from darkness to light, and from the power of Satan to*

*God, that they may receive forgiveness of sins and an inheritance among those who are sanctified by faith in Me."* (Acts 26:12–18)

On the road to Damascus, Saul, now Paul, was given a new cornerstone upon which he was to build the foundation of his life. No longer was he to pursue the persecution of Christians. Now, as a Christian himself, he was called to pursue the salvation of Jews and Gentiles alike. Because of this vision from the Lord, his foundation and life course changed as the Lord transformed him from a persecutor to prophet, from a mocker to a missionary.

*Therefore, King Agrippa, I was not disobedient to the heavenly vision, but declared first to those in Damascus and in Jerusalem, and throughout all the region of Judea, and then to the Gentiles, that they should repent, turn to God, and do works befitting repentance. For these reasons the Jews seized me in the temple and tried to kill me. Therefore, having obtained help from God, to this day I stand, witnessing both to small and great, saying no other things than those which the prophets and Moses said would come; that the Christ would suffer, that He would be the first to rise from the dead, and would proclaim light to the Jewish people and to the Gentiles.* (Acts 26:19–23)

Now, the truth of the matter is that Paul's vision was quite dramatic. He not only audibly heard Christ speak but also was temporarily blinded by a heavenly flash of light. (See Acts 22:6–10.) Can we expect our visions to be the same? Are we guaranteed to see lights from heaven? I think it's safe to say no. While it's true that some visions may be pronounced and dramatic, not all of them will be. The litmus test for a godly vision is not the sounds or sights that accompany it but rather its faithfulness to God's Word. God may choose to communicate in dramatic ways, but He also chooses to speak in the quiet.

Dr. Myles Munroe, in his book *The Principles and Power of Vision,* defines *vision* as "foresight with insight based on hindsight." He writes:

> We have insight into God's purpose for us based on what we know God has already accomplished in eternity. Vision is a glimpse of our future that God has purposed. We don't know all the details of how our purposes will unfold, but we see their "ends" because God reveals them to us in the visions He gives us. This is why we can be confident that they will come to pass. [3]

You'll know a vision is from God when it fits with His Scripture, when it furthers His kingdom, and when His glory is the chief goal. Visions may not be as pronounced in our lives as Paul's was in his, but they are still the cornerstones for our solid foundations, just as Paul's vision was the cornerstone for his foundation of ministry. God calls us to lay the foundations in our lives around godly visions, whatever realm these foundations may be in.

> A vision is from God when His glory is the chief goal.

# First Cathedral: Modern-Day Vision at Work

The vision upon which my foundation was built has been with me for as long as I can remember. Very early in

3. Dr. Myles Munroe, *The Principles and Power of Vision,* (New Kensington: Whitaker House, 2003), 43.

life, I came to believe in a great God who could not fail at anything, and, at the tender age of ten, I preached my very first sermon. It took place during evening church on the third Sunday in June of 1956 at the Golden Leaf Missionary Baptist Church in Memphis, Tennessee. I will never forget that day. Although I was only a child, I was already dreaming that, one day, I would lead a great congregation—and, more specifically, a congregation that reflected racial and social unity.

## A Backdrop of Discord and Disunity

I remember in 1968 when the Rev. Dr. Martin Luther King Jr. came to Memphis to support a garbage workers' strike, just prior to his death. The garbage workers labored for long hours with no overtime or sick pay. They were so underpaid that even those who worked full-time still qualified to receive state welfare. There were some white workers, but, for the most part, they drove the trucks and were not required to actually pick up the trash. That was reserved for the black workers.

Many thought this strike was nothing more than a racial matter, but it wasn't hard to see that it was actually about economic survival, class struggle, and social intolerance. As a child, I couldn't help but notice how the rich were treated with far greater respect than the poor, while the poor were often used and abused, overworked and underpaid. The rich *were* becoming richer, and the poor *were* becoming poorer, although in this case it had nothing to do with lack of effort on the part of the poor.

In response to this social injustice, many began building ministries whose primary cause was to minister to the poor and disenfranchised. This was commendable, and, through this effort, many people were reached with the Gospel and churches grew. I chose not to take the same route, however, believing that, if I did, I would perpetuate the same separatist mentality. Segregation practiced by the poor was just as bad as segregation practiced by the rich. My vision was to rise above segregation by building a congregation that would reflect all elements of society—rich and poor, black and white, men and women alike.

I truly believed that many people from different backgrounds could live together peacefully and—even more importantly—worship God together. After all, on that first Day of Pentecost, people of many nations were in Jerusalem when God rewarded the disciples for patiently awaiting the arrival of *"another Helper"* (John 14:16), God's Holy Spirit. Though culturally different, all the people there were *"with one accord,"* as Luke's account in Acts makes clear: *"When the Day of Pentecost had fully come, they were all with one accord in one place"* (Acts 2:1).

In other words, not only were these varied people together, but they were also in agreement. They stood side by side not only in body but also in spirit. And this is what I desired and longed for in the congregation that I believed God was leading me to pastor. I knew that, within the church of Jesus Christ, many nationalities and races could live in harmony as one. And, even as racial unrest seemed to increase in the South, I envisioned a church that would respond only to the color of love. I knew then, as a young boy, what I was called to bring about, and I determined to live my life in constant pursuit of that call. It was this cornerstone vision that prompted my laying of a solid ministry foundation.

## The Vision Realized

Because of the Lord's many blessings over the years, our congregation is flourishing today—both in numbers and in spiritual growth. The vision has been realized and continues to be realized more each day. God has prospered our work to include a preschool, an elementary school, a Bible college, and more than seventy active ministries, either within the church or through outreaches to the surrounding communities. Praise God for the ministry He has built around the cornerstone He placed in my life so many years ago.

## Sticking to the Vision...

Remember our definition for *cornerstone* as found in *The American Heritage Dictionary*? It was, "A stone at the corner of a building uniting two intersecting walls." [4] Well, there's another definition, too, and it goes as follows: "Such a stone, often inscribed, laid at a ceremony marking the origin of a building." [5] Maybe you've seen such stones before. It's not unusual for churches or businesses to place a stone like this near their main entrance, noting the year their congregation or business began and the year their building was erected. Such stones serve as memorials and reminders of beginnings. They draw our attention back to the initial vision, back to the main reason and purpose for undertaking the building project that has now been completed.

> A cornerstone is crucial in reminding you of God's vision for your life.

It's important for you to have reminder cornerstones like this in your life. As you lay your solid foundation and build up your life, you are bound to face discouragement and distraction. In these times, a cornerstone is crucial for renewing your thoughts and reminding yourself of the vision God has called you to pursue.

---

4. *The American Heritage® Dictionary of the English Language,* 4th ed., s.v. "cornerstone."
5. Ibid.

## ...Through the Trials...

Times of discouragement are bound to come as you begin laying your foundation around your vision cornerstone. Paul, whose ministry was characterized by one discouraging situation after another, provides a perfect example. Read again his defense to King Agrippa:

*Therefore, King Agrippa, I was not disobedient to the heavenly vision, but declared first to those in Damascus and in Jerusalem, and throughout all the region of Judea, and then to the Gentiles, that they should repent, turn to God, and do works befitting repentance. For these reasons the Jews seized me in the temple and tried to kill me. Therefore, having obtained help from God, to this day I stand, witnessing both to small and great, saying no other things than those which the prophets and Moses said would come; that the Christ would suffer, that He would be the first to rise from the dead, and would proclaim light to the Jewish people and to the Gentiles.* (Acts 26:19–23)

Notice Paul's attitude. Even though *"the Jews seized [him] in the temple and tried to kill [him]"* (v. 21), he continued in his mission, faithfully pursuing the vision God had entrusted to him. How did he do this? First, he remembered his vision: *"I was not disobedient to the heavenly vision, but declared first to those in Damascus and in Jerusalem, and throughout all the region of Judea, and then to the Gentiles, that they should repent, turn to God, and do works befitting repentance"* (vv. 19–20). He laid down a reminder cornerstone and turned to it often in times of trial so as to keep his life on track. Second, Paul sought and received help from his God, the Author of his vision:

*Having obtained help from God, to this day I stand, witnessing both to small and great, saying no other things than those which the prophets and Moses said would come; that the Christ would suffer, that He would be the first to rise from the dead, and would proclaim light to the Jewish people and to the Gentiles.* (Acts 26: 22–23)

Times of trial will certainly come. Have you laid down your reminder cornerstone?

## ...And Through the Temptations...

Discouragement is not the only threat as we lay foundations in our lives. Distractions can cause difficulties, too, as we are tempted to turn our attention away from our initial God-given vision toward self-focused visions along the way. Let me give you an example.

Our experience at The First Cathedral is not in any way unique. Outreaches such as ours, which focus on uniting people from many backgrounds, races, and social standings, have become commonplace in many cities throughout the United States and the world. Often, tremendous church growth is present in these churches, resulting in what Pentecostal historian Vinson Synan terms "free-standing mega-churches." [6] Even though the church I lead may rightly fit into this "mega-church" category, I have always preferred to refer to our assembly as simply a church.

It can be very tempting to become distracted by the excitement of church growth and, as a result, lose sight of the initial vision. Whether or not a church reaches "mega" status may be totally irrelevant to the purpose for which

6. Vinson Synan, *The Century of the Holy Spirit: 100 Years of Pentecostal and Charismatic Renewal, 1901–2001,* (Nashville: Thomas Nelson Publishers, 2001), 373.

God birthed it. Throughout the world, churches of all sizes and varied affiliations are buying buildings, starting Christian schools, pioneering substance abuse programs, establishing feeding programs for the desperate of their communities, rescuing unwed mothers and unwanted children, and serving as employment agencies for those who are out of work. God is able to work through each of these churches as they are faithful to the initial vision God gave them—not to a secondary distracting vision. Churches—both large and small—have had opportunities to make a major difference in their communities as they labor to fulfill the Great Commission of our Lord.

It would be naïve and unwise of me to deny the power of exponential growth within a church. Growth has happened and continues to happen to us, and I am thankful to God for it. But growth for growth's sake has never been my primary focus. There are valuable underlying principles that have guided us to this point of increase, and principles such as these are essential to any endeavor in life. As a church, we first had to lay a solid foundation. Then, as we laid this foundation, we had to continually remind ourselves of the cornerstone of our growth—our initial vision. Discouragement and distraction came, but we remembered the vision and the Author of the vision. Discouragement will come your way in life, as will distraction. Make sure you've laid the cornerstone for a solid foundation in your life, and you will be equipped to handle these obstacles.

# Chapter Three
# Change: Good or Bad?

The Lord eventually planted my ministry in New England, which has often been referred to as "a preacher's graveyard." Needless to say, I found myself facing a host of unique challenges, such as the suspicion with which many New Englanders regard pastors and other spiritual figures. Noted author and pastor Gordon MacDonald expressed these challenges well in his afterword to Stephan A. Macchia's book *Becoming a Healthy Church*. In reference to statements he often heard, such as, "New England is a burned-out area; churches can't grow here" and "It might happen in Florida, but it will never happen here," MacDonald wrote the following: "A quarter for every time I heard those comments would have made me a rich man by now." [1]

It was true. Over the years, I watched as hundreds of New England pastors became discouraged and quit.

---

1. Gordon MacDonald, afterword to *Becoming a Healthy Church: 10 Characteristics*, by Stephen A. Macchia (Grand Rapids: Baker Books, 1999), 223.

But I wasn't about to quit. The failures I witnessed only challenged me to get closer to God, and He used this trying time to teach me how to hear His voice more clearly. As I listened to Him, He impressed upon my heart the need for change, for new vision, and for a unique strategy to win the hearts of these people to whom He had sent me to minister. I became convinced that if something had not already been done, it was not because it could not be done, but because the right approach just hadn't been tried yet. If I had insisted on using the same approaches that everyone else in the area used, our ministry would certainly have suffered the same fate as theirs. If we wanted to experience change in the region, then we, too, had to change. With the right changes, I was certain growth would come.

This presented our ministry with a whole new challenge. New Englanders are slow to embrace change, and they hold anything that becomes too large up to serious scrutiny . How well would they handle my newfangled attempts to establish a church, much less a church that might grow? If I were to take an arrogant, heavy-handed approach, demanding that changes be made, I surely would fail. At the same time, if I were to take a completely conciliatory approach, simply trying to please others in my community, I would be perceived as weak, and no one wants a weak, wishy-washy leader. In the end, I found myself walking a tightrope between placating the people in my new community and implementing the changes that I knew were essential. It was a tough balancing act, and only by the grace of God was I able to see it through.

At the same time that I was dealing with this challenge, I found myself wrestling with another issue. How, I wondered, do I reconcile this need for change with the changeless nature of God? Malachi 3:6 says, *"For I am the*

LORD, *I do not change."* And Hebrews 13:8 reads, *"Jesus Christ is the same yesterday, today, and forever."* If we are called to be like God, and we know God to be eternally constant and never-changing, then how can we embrace change so readily? Is it inconsistent with our call to mirror Him in all that we do?

I knew that God was calling me toward change. In fact, I knew that God Himself often made changes: *"Behold, I will do a new thing, now it shall spring forth"* (Isaiah 43:19). Just because God's *nature* was changeless didn't mean His *methods* would always be the same. Throughout the Old and New Testaments, God was continually surprising His people by doing the

> God continually surprises His people by doing the unexpected.

unexpected. Who would have ever thought God would come to earth as a man? That was a new one! Although God Himself is eternally the same, it's clear that He often uses new methods and means to communicate with His people.

But I still found myself tied up in a philosophical and theological knot. How do you differentiate, I wondered, between change that's good and change that's bad? While I knew change was necessary for our ministry at that point, certainly change for change's sake wasn't the approach to take. We couldn't start embracing all changes simply *because* they were changes. A more balanced approach was definitely needed. I finally found it, but first I had a lot of learning to do.

## Change or Die

There's a famous poem by E. A. Robinson called *Miniver Cheevy* about a man who so longed for days of old that he became completely disconnected from life around him.

The poem explains that Miniver Cheevy so hated time's progression that he "assailed," or attacked and cursed, the changing of seasons. This is the epitome of resistance to change. As the poem reveals, this man was so reluctant to live in the now that he buried himself in escapist daydreams, imagining himself to be a knight, just so he wouldn't have to face the present day.

Have you ever met a Miniver Cheevy, someone who's so resistant to change that he or she clings to the good old days at all costs? Maybe, on an issue dear to your heart, the Miniver-mentality has even made appearances in *your* life. What realms of your life are you most protective of? Are there certain areas in which you simply will not allow change, no matter how convincing an argument you might hear for the benefits of implementing change in those areas? Change has never been easy, and our minds often tend to reject it. Change is inevitable, however, and we must learn not only to accept it but also to embrace it. It is necessary for growth: emotionally, spiritually, financially, and socially. A refusal to change will quickly render us obsolete and ineffectual as our ever-changing world spins ahead without us.

> We must learn not only to accept change but also to embrace it.

I learned the importance of change several years ago when I purchased my first laptop computer. At the time, it was at the top of the line. Before the year had even ended, however, salespeople were calling me and trying to convince me to upgrade my software. This annoyed me; I thought my programs suited my needs just fine. I ignored their insistence to upgrade and kept plugging away on my original software.

Then, something happened. As time progressed, so did my needs, and with these new needs came new demands—demands that my current computer setup clearly could not handle. In the end, I had to swallow my pride, call the salespeople, and upgrade my software. If I wanted to be relevant and effective, I simply had to change.

The bottom line is that change is inevitable. Do you listen to the same music, wear the same hairstyle, sport the same clothes, and use the same slang expressions that your parents did at your age? Most likely, no. From architecture to tax law to technology, change is something we can expect. In instances such as these, it's safe to say that accepting the change is the best way to go.

But what about the issues where it's not so safe to change? On a national level, for instance, should we, as Christians, embrace the changing view of life our nation has come to accept since *Roe v. Wade*? In our churches, should we embrace a new worship service format or a new Bible translation as eagerly and unquestioningly as we embrace a new pair of shoes? Or in the workplace, should we buy the newest technological toys and employ the latest management styles simply for the sake of newness and change, without ever evaluating their necessity or effectiveness?

These are sticky situations. After considering the above examples, I think you'll agree that change must always be accompanied by careful, prayerful thinking.

## The Cornerstone Test

During my own times of prayer and thinking about change, I arrived at what I like to call The Cornerstone Test. It's not foolproof, and it's not guaranteed to make every decision quick, easy, and clear-cut. Perhaps, however, you'll find it to be a good starting point as you take on the task of evaluating change in your own life, and for that reason, I share it here.

The Cornerstone Test has two parts:

1. *Will this change bring me closer to attaining my vision in this specific situation?* Does this change fit into the cornerstone that God has already led me to lay for my life? (See chapter 2.)

2. *Will this change bring me closer to attaining my ultimate vision, that of glorifying Jesus Christ in all that I do?* (See 1 Corinthians 10:31.) Is this change in keeping with the standards of my ultimate Cornerstone, Jesus Christ?

## Part One: Will This Change Bring Me Closer to My Specific Vision?

This part of The Cornerstone Test is easy to understand but not always easy to implement. In this part of the test, the change is evaluated from a practical standpoint. For example, imagine that you are a department manager at your workplace and your vision, or goal, is to increase overall department productivity. In a recent business journal, you read an advertisement for the latest "Power Productivity Plan," an online correspondence course that teaches employees time-management techniques and imparts time-saving tips. You think about it some and realize, "The Power Productivity Plan may bring me closer to my vision of increased productivity." Do you immediately call the listed 1-800 number and sign up all your employees for training? The hasty manager might, but with The Cornerstone Test, more information is needed.

So, you do a little more research. You call the 1-800 number, but not to sign up all your employees. Instead, you ask for an informational package to be mailed to you so you can learn more about the program. You then go online, do an Internet search for "Power Productivity Plan," and read what other users have to say about the product. You immediately discover something that makes your jaw drop. The Power Productivity Plan requires *six full months of all-day training*! Even worse, the minimum employee requirement for training packages is ten people. You only have eleven employees in your department to begin with! If you sign up ten of your employees to take online classes all day, every day, for the next six months, that will leave your office horribly understaffed. Will the Power Productivity Plan really bring you closer to your specific goal of employee productivity? Probably not. After research, you've come to realize that the trade-off is not worth it—all the time-management techniques and time-saving tips in the world can hardly compensate for the time you'll lose by signing up your employees for six months of time-consuming training.

After prayerfully and carefully thinking through the possible change before you, you realize that the Power Productivity Plan will not bring you closer to your desired goal of department productivity, after all. With peace of mind, you abandon that plan and keep looking for other options.

This is part one of The Cornerstone Test at its simplest. In real life, you may find yourself having to evaluate your proposed change through the lens of The Cornerstone Test several times over. I encourage you to stick with it. Evaluate and reevaluate and reevaluate some more. If a change takes you *away* from your goal instead of *toward* it, the change is not worth making.

### Part Two: Will This Change Bring Me Closer to My Ultimate Vision?

Part two of The Cornerstone Test is where you bring your Bible out as your ultimate reference book and guide. Scripture repeatedly refers to Jesus as *"the chief cornerstone."* For example, 1 Peter 2:6 reads, *"Therefore it is also contained in the Scripture, 'Behold, I lay in Zion a chief cornerstone, elect, precious, and he who believes on Him will by no means be put to shame.'"* (See also Matthew 21:42, Mark 12:10, Luke 20:17, and Acts 4:11.)

Jesus is the Chief Cornerstone of all that we do. We must remember that, as His children, glorifying Him is our ultimate goal. All endeavors that we undertake—whether they be remodeling our houses, enriching our minds through education, building businesses from the ground up, or establishing new ministries in our churches—are within the context of a larger endeavor, that of the Christian race. As a Christian, glorifying Christ must be my chief aim, driving my every action. *"I press on, that I may lay hold of that for which Christ Jesus has also laid hold of me"* (Philippians 3:12). Any change that does not line up with Christ our Cornerstone is too costly to make.

## The Sum of the Matter

The long and short of it is that we can expect to face change in our lives. Whether with fashion or friends, in the workplace or at home, by ourselves or in a group, we can count on change and anticipate transformation. The question is, How will we respond? Will we reject the change too quickly, out of fear and apprehension? Doing so may leave us like Miniver Cheevy, who, at the poem's end, is found drowning his sorrows in a lonely drink at the bar. Or, in an attempt to avoid the Miniver-mentality at all costs, will we unthinkingly and unquestioningly embrace change in our hungry search for something new? Both of these reactions are extreme ways to handle change, and the wise response lies somewhere in the middle. It is my prayer that you will carefully and prayerfully think through change in your own life and endeavors.

# Chapter Four
# Treading the Trails of Tradition

O ur discussion on change would be incomplete without turning to the topic of tradition. *Tradition* is a word fraught with connotations, both good and bad. For some, the word evokes a sense of entrapment, stuffiness, and extreme ineffectiveness. "Out with the old, in with the new," is the mantra for these folks, and they quickly chuck anything that has even a tinge of tradition. For others, *tradition* is a comforting word, conjuring feelings of contentment, nostalgia, and safety. These are the "If-it's-good-enough-for-Mom-and-Dad-then-it's-good-enough-for-me" folks, and they cling to even the most nonsensical traditions, simply for the sake of keeping the old ways around.

My guess is that you fall somewhere between these two extremes on the tradition spectrum. Wherever you are, though, you are bound to encounter others in life who are at slightly different spots on the tradition scale, and this has the potential to end in some head-butting. For this reason, carefully considering what Scripture has to say about tradition is important when laying your foundation.

# The "Wows" of Tradition

No matter where you stand on the tradition spectrum, "wow" is probably not the first word that comes to mind when someone mentions tradition. Instead, you probably think of terms like "tried and true," "stable," "steady," "constant." But never, "wow"—a word that suggests excitement and new discovery. In reality, though, tradition really is a thing of wonder and wow.

In the church, most prominently in the Catholic Church, there is the tradition of Lent. Lent includes the forty days before Easter, which are reserved as a time for fasting, discipline, self-denial, and reflection on the sufferings that Christ endured during His time on earth, particularly in the days leading up to and including the Crucifixion. It is a solemn season on the church's calendar, and many people avoid it because of the sadness it embodies or because of the rituals that are often part of its celebration. Some may think of it as nothing more than an unnecessary and very depressing religious tradition.

However, as Pastor Ken Collins points out, the tradition of Lent can be a powerful tool to remind us of the joys that we, as Christians, have in Christ our Lord, who conquered death, disease, darkness, and depression. In his essay, "Honest to God," Collins writes,

> We avoid Lent and Holy Week because it isn't a happy and uplifting time—but to be honest, neither is most of life....The people of this world believe in the power of positive thinking and in happiness, and in believing these things, they are very shrewd. For people of this world have only the present moment, and if they are unhappy in it, they have lost something. But we who are Christians can endure unhappiness and sadness and loneliness

and backstabbing and betrayal and friendlessness and poverty and hunger and thirst; we can face mourning and grief and even death, because Jesus faced all those things. As Christians, we know that Jesus' suffering was His way to glory, and His Crucifixion was the door to His Resurrection. We know that He ascended on high and sits, alive and well, at the right hand of His Father, where He rules over all things. We can face our own crucifixions in life, because we know that we will share in His Resurrection on the Last Day! [1]

We are reminded that the tradition of Lent, even with all its intricate rites, ceremonies, and formalities, truly can inspire wonder, amazement, awe, and wow. Encapsulated in those forty days is a time for Christians to identify with the sufferings of their Lord Jesus Christ. Lent can serve as a time of refocusing attention away from ourselves and onto God. And most wonderful of all, it is a time of anticipation for Easter, which mirrors the even greater anticipation that we, as Christians, possess as we expectantly look forward to our Lord's return. *"For the earnest expectation of the creation eagerly waits for the revealing of the sons of God"* (Romans 8:19). All of this is wrapped up in that "stuffy old tradition"!

So, tradition can be a most excellent thing. A host of Christian traditions have proven themselves to be fruitful and fulfilling. For example, attending church services on Sundays is a tradition many Christian believers all over the world have adopted. Nowhere in Scripture are we commanded to pick Sunday as our meeting day, yet we have come to accept Sunday—the first day of the week and

1. Kenneth W. Collins, "Honest to God," © 2003. <http://www.KenCollins.com> (31 March, 2003)

the day of our Lord's resurrection—as the day that we set aside for worship, our Sabbath. This has proven itself to be an honorable tradition, as well as a reminder to believers that the Lord deserves our best and our first in everything, even when it comes down to deciding on which day of the week we will gather to worship.

Celebrating special holidays like wedding anniversaries, birthdays, Thanksgiving, and Christmas are not clearly mandated in Scripture either, yet the tradition of meeting for these festive occasions provides us with great opportunities to share quality time with the people we love. Family traditions can be rewarding, too, as they draw us together for family meals, special celebrations, and routine gatherings. Truly, tradition can be a blessing.

## The "Woes" of Tradition

Even for all its blessings, however, tradition has the potential to turn into a ball and chain. This happens whenever we value a tradition itself over the principle it embodies. For example, in many cultures, arranged marriages are a long-standing tradition. In such societies, parents are responsible for finding and securing a mate for their child. The rationale behind this tradition is that parents, understanding both the personality of their child and the nature of the marriage relationship, are better equipped to make decisions about marriage than their child is. The truth is that many planned marriages end up being quite strong, happy, and fulfilling. But what happens when a son or daughter begins loving someone whom their parents have not planned for their child to marry? Should the parents immediately prohibit the relationship solely on the grounds that they have not arranged it? Shouldn't they first take time to become acquainted with their son's or daughter's love interest and then decide if they would like to give their stamp of approval or not? Hopefully they would choose this second option, since the ultimate goal is a successful marriage and the happiness of their child. To prohibit what could be a very good marriage, merely for the sake of adhering to the arranged marriage tradition, would be tragic.

Tradition is only as good as the intended purpose that it helps us to attain. Nineteenth century British Prime Minister Benjamin Disraeli once said, "A precedent embalms a principle." [2] In other words, a precedent—or tradition—is meant to preserve and protect our principles and goals. However, when we forget our goals and continue to hold on to the precedent itself, even when that precedent doesn't bring us an inch closer to our goals, warning bells should start to sound.

For another example, consider the typewriter. In its time, the typewriter was a wonderful laborsaving device, a very effective tool. It was used widely to record information, compile books, and write newspaper articles. As an alternative to the tedious task of handwriting, typing was an attractive time-saving option. Although some people had trouble getting the hang of this "new-fangled writing-machine" [3] (Mark Twain "declared it was ruining his morals—that it made him 'want to swear'" [4]), others embraced it as a quicker, more convenient means of communication.

With the advent of word processors and personal computers, however, the typewriter soon became obsolete. No longer were there extreme limitations on font type and

2. Brainy Quotes. <http://www.brainyquote.com/quotes/quotes/b/q134337.html> (9 April, 2003)

3. *Mark Twain: A Biography by Albert Bigelow Paine,* (New York: Harper & Brothers, 1912), 535–538.

4. Ibid.

size or on placement of the text. The sky was now the limit when it came to text appearance! And no longer did a person have to blot out errors with a messy correction fluid. He or she could simply press "delete." Tradition gave way to efficiency.

## What Does the Bible Say?

There are several Scripture passages that shed a lot of light on the topic of tradition. One is found in Matthew 15, where Jesus challenged the scribes' and Pharisees' understanding of tradition. These teachers of the Law approached Jesus and asked Him, *"Why do Your disciples transgress the tradition of the elders? For they do not wash their hands when they eat bread"* (v. 2). What followed was a very enlightening conversation:

> *He answered and said to them, "Why do you also transgress the commandment of God because of your tradition? For God commanded, saying, 'Honor your father and your mother'; and, 'He who curses father or mother, let him be put to death.' But you say, 'Whoever says to his father or mother, "Whatever profit you might have received from me is a gift to God"; then he need not honor his father or mother.' Thus you have made the commandment of God of no effect by your tradition. Hypocrites! Well did Isaiah prophesy about you, saying: 'These people draw near to Me with their mouth, and honor Me with their lips, but their heart is far from Me. And in vain they worship Me, teaching as doctrines the commandments of men.'"* (Matthew 15:3–9)

Jesus got to the heart of the matter. When the scribes and Pharisees asked Him why His disciples didn't follow

58

tradition, Jesus turned the tables and started questioning *them*. "Why," He essentially asked, "Why do you disobey God for the sake of man-made tradition?" Jesus' words must have hit home for the Pharisees. Look at their reaction just a few verses later: *"Then His disciples came and said to Him, 'Do You know that the Pharisees were offended when they heard this saying?'"* (v. 12). Perhaps the Pharisees, convicted but unwilling to repent, knew deep down that obedience to God really was the more important issue.

We learn a key lesson about tradition from this Bible passage, and it is this: God finds vain tradition appalling. Tradition in and of itself can be a useful tool for worshipping God more fully, and God has no problem with tradition per se. However, when tradition leads us into praising God with our mouths while our hearts remain distant, it is deplorable to our Lord. *"And in vain they worship me, teaching as doctrines the commandments of men"* (v. 9).

What does it mean to worship *"in vain"*? Merriam-Webster defines *vain* as "having no real value: idle, worthless; marked by futility or ineffectualness: unsuccessful, useless." [5] In other words, something done "in vain" is a failed attempt to reach a certain goal. This describes well many of our Christian traditions, things that are not bad in and of themselves but that better served a former generation—not our own. When we worship "in vain," we *try* to worship, but we end up missing the mark because our actions do not achieve the ultimate goal of glorifying Christ. The only way to ensure that our worship—or anything else in our lives—is done in truth and not in vain is to evaluate it and examine whether it helps achieve our goals and aims or hinders them. All traditions that do

5. *Merriam-Webster's Collegiate Dictionary*, Electronic Edition, Version 1.1, s.v. "vain."

not bring us closer to God's ultimate aims are empty traditions that deserve to be tossed; conversely, any traditions that move us toward His goals and aims should be embraced and encouraged.

My spiritual heritage is one that I consider rich, and I have always been very proud of it. Within my heritage, however, I have seen many good ministries die because the church or its leadership refused to change enough to be relevant to an ever-changing world. I have watched many men die spiritually because they valued their traditions over their call to reach and touch hurting souls with the Gospel of Christ. Ministry for them became a rigid ritual rather than a flow from the Holy Spirit that could be changed at any moment, as God desired, and as God mandated.

I realized very early in my ministry that just because something had been done a certain way in the past didn't make it right or even establish it as the best and only way things could be done. My ministerial future depended on my ability to use what I had learned from God's Word, and what I had experienced in my life, translating the sum total of it into a language the average person of my time could understand. Insisting that everything be done as it had been done for years, decades, or even centuries would have meant death for my ministry.

Although I have always had a profound respect for the many leaders and ministers who helped shape me into what I am, I have also realized that any such persons are just part of God's molding process. Because of the greatness of what God wants to do in me, His plan far exceeds the ability of any one individual to make me into what I need to be. Therefore, I must not look to the traditions of any man but only unto God Himself.

## One More Bible Story...

When Moses, the great deliverer and leader of the Hebrew nation, died, God did not require that his replacement, Joshua, celebrate all the traditions of his predecessor. It's true that Joshua had learned many valuable leadership lessons from Moses, his mentor. He had watched Moses lead Israel through some of the most trying times in its history and had witnessed Moses under great pressure. He saw how Moses responded to tough times and how he sprang back from disappointment, even amid the people's complaints that he lacked the ability to lead and hear from God.

> Many leaders let their loyalty to tradition overshadow a much-needed message God has for today.

Interestingly enough, however, God didn't mourn Moses' death, nor did he advise Joshua to do so.

> *After the death of Moses the servant of the LORD, it came to pass that the LORD spoke to Joshua the son of Nun, Moses' assistant, saying: "Moses My servant is dead. Now therefore, arise, go over this Jordan, you and all this people, to the land which I am giving to them; the children of Israel."*
>
> (Joshua 1:1–2)

Moses had served his generation well, and now it was time for Joshua to do the same. He could not fully obey God by celebrating the traditions of Moses, for that would be dishonoring the voice of God to him at that moment. God's voice for the present always takes precedence over obeying past traditions.

Tragically, many leaders today are not as wise as Joshua was. They often feel a need to be so loyal to traditions of the past that they ultimately fail to see a much-needed message God is trying to convey to them for the here and now. Don't get me wrong; we should never minimize God's working throughout history. What God did through another person at another time is wonderful, and we should reflect on such situations with awe at God's perfect work in His children throughout all of history. We are not, however, exempt from hearing His voice in the present.

We must beware of traditions that may hinder our ability to hear what God is saying right here, right now. If God is trying to reorganize your ministry, your business, or your relationship, and you continue to say, "This is how we have always done it," you limit God's potential for building anything of lasting value in your life. God desires to build vision within us, but this can only happen when we are open-minded and open-spirited enough to accept the words He has for each new day.

Had Joshua been closed-minded to his future and the changes he would have to embrace, he may never have crossed the Jordan River. Had he been closed-spirited to the possibilities of God's tomorrows, he may have ignored the beautiful blueprint God was drawing up for his new life. Praise God that Joshua wasn't closed-minded or closed-spirited, but was instead eager and excited to accept God's leading for his life. Joshua was greatly rewarded, for the Lord promised him guidance and assurance all the days of his life. Although Joshua had to leave behind many traditions and ways of doing things, he didn't have to leave behind his God. The same God who had led him thus far promised to protect and direct him in all he was yet to undertake.

> God desires to build vision within us, but we must accept the words He has for each new day.

*No man shall be able to stand before you all the days of your life; as I was with Moses, so I will be with you. I will not leave you nor forsake you. Be strong and of good courage, for to this people you shall divide as an inheritance the land which I swore to their fathers to give them.* (Joshua 1:5–6)

Are you ready to let vain traditions die so that the glory of your Lord can shine forth in your life today? Or are you clinging to what's comfortable at the cost of tasting the new mercies of your eternal, unchanging Lord? It is my prayer that you will embrace tradition when it needs to be embraced and reject it when it deserves rejection. Overall, remember to embrace and obey your Lord in every moment.

# Chapter Five
# Clearing the Land: Whose Responsibility Is It?

---

**B**efore a foundation can be laid, the land has to be cleared. Any other structures on the land must be leveled, trees must be cut down, and any rocks and boulders must be removed. Only then, once all these intrusive—and possibly destructive—distractions are out of the way, can a builder break ground, get down to business, and start laying his structural foundation. With these things in the way, however, the builder is not able to make an inch of progress toward laying the foundation.

Let's suppose your neighbor—we'll call him Bob—decides he wants to build a new house from the ground up. After you finish mowing your lawn one summer afternoon, you peek your head over the fence that separates his yard from yours and casually ask him how his new home is progressing. "Pretty good," he says, "although we've hit a few speed bumps." You express your condolences, wish him improved success, and then ask him what the problem is. "Now, tell me again," you ask, "Where are you building?" Your neighbor raises his eyebrows at you, obviously confused. "What do you mean, where am I building? Right here, of course!" Now you're the confused one! How can Bob build a house where a house is already standing? No wonder he's been hitting speed bumps! He needs to tear down his old house before he can start building a new one in its place.

The same truth holds for our lives, as well. Often we try building where faulty foundations have already been laid, refusing to take the time necessary to unearth these crumbling walls that will only impede our attempts at progress and development. The reasons are numerous: We don't have time to rip up the old foundation, we're emotionally attached to it, or we're just too lazy to tackle what seems like an insurmountable project.

Or maybe you don't have an old foundation that you're trying to build around; you just face a lot of trees, rocks, and uneven ground. But instead of taking time out to clear and level the land, you just start building. What results is a crooked foundation with all kinds of cracks and leaks because of the roots and boulders you neglected to remove. Again, your reasons for not taking care of these obstacles may be numerous. Whatever your reasons, though, they're certainly not good enough if your brand new house is sure to crumble and collapse in no time at all.

# Building Points:
## Where to Start the Digging

Does this strike a chord with you? Have you found yourself staring, amazed and befuddled, at your friends, neighbors, acquaintances, and family members as you've witnessed them trying to build without first clearing the land. Maybe it's the girl in your church who's expressed a new eagerness to serve Jesus Christ but still won't consider leaving the non-Christian boyfriend who mocks her every time she talks about God. Perhaps it's the coworker who complains about his weight yet continues to have two burgers, french fries, and a chocolate shake for lunch every day. Or maybe it's the family member who constantly complains about the messy house he has to put up with when, all the while, *he's* the one leaving dirty socks, candy wrappers, pop cans, and half-eaten

> We can get so caught up in identifying the wrong in other people's lives that we forget to look at our own.

bowls of cereal on every available surface. We don't understand it when we see behavior like this. How can a person have a desire but continue carrying out a lifestyle totally contrary to attaining that desire?

But wait a second: Before you hunt down this person to give him or her a talking-to about clearing their land, take stock of your own life. Are you trying to build around roots and rocks? Are you ignoring the uneven ground and old foundations in your own life?

> *And why do you look at the speck in your brother's eye, but do not consider the plank in your own eye? Or how can you say to your brother, "Let me remove the speck from your eye"; and look, a plank is in your own eye? Hypocrite! First remove the plank from your own eye, and then you will see clearly to remove the speck from your brother's eye.*
> (Matthew 7:3–5)

Jesus' message is clear. Often we get so caught up in identifying what's wrong in other people's lives that we forget to look at our own. This is one of the not-so-flattering tendencies of human nature. Somehow we're always able to find problems in others while still managing to overlook our own shortcomings. And whenever our lives *do* come under the microscope, we're quick to make excuses for our behavior and slow to admit our need for improvement.

Yet, as Jesus taught us, this is completely opposite from how we should be living. We need to examine ourselves first—by unearthing the rocks, roots, and boulders that are crowding the "land" of our lives—before we even offer a word of advice to our neighbors.

Maybe you're familiar with the saying that whatever we most dislike in others is often identifiable in our own characters. In other words, we are most bothered by the things in other people that remind us of ourselves. As a result, most of us spend a great deal of time trying to change others to fit a model we envision for them. Whenever we do this, I believe that we are actually trying to escape the reality of our own insufficiencies. We draw attention to others, hoping to draw attention away from our own flaws. In effect, we say, "Don't look at me, because if you keep looking, you just might discover that I have problems even greater than yours." As long as we can keep attention focused on others and off ourselves, we're safe.

This ultimately leads to a lifetime of disguise. We're afraid to let others see the "real" us, and so, as we direct attention toward others, we simultaneously sculpt intricate masks for ourselves. Is this any way to live? I think you'd agree with me that a lifetime of mask-wearing would be not only difficult but also unfulfilling. How enjoyable would life be if you were constantly asking yourself, "Now, what does he *really* mean by that?" or "What is she *really* feeling?" How content would you be in knowing that others have grown to love your mask, not the real you?

# Pick Up the Shovel and Get to Work

The entire process of building a solid foundation—from leveling the land and removing obstructions to breaking ground and laying the first foundation stone—is nobody's responsibility but your own. Just as you are not primarily responsible for the speck in your neighbor's eye, he is not primarily responsible for the plank in yours. It is *your* job to pick up a shovel and get to work. And this often means being brutally honest about who you are.

## Removing the Mask

This is the first step. Before you can build a lasting foundation in your life, you must know who you are. Like a builder, you must familiarize yourself with the land. Just as a builder needs to know what type of soil he's building on and what kind of construction tools and materials he'll be using, you need to be intimately acquainted with who you are. Building without this foundational information could end in disastrous results—like the pile of sawdust that would no doubt result if someone built a stick house in prime tornado country.

> Before you can build a lasting foundation, you must know who you are.

How do you get to know who you are? By removing your mask. This isn't always easy, and we definitely need help in this process. Pray that the Lord would lead you into understanding more fully who you are—faults, foibles, failures, and all. Honesty is key. Openly recognize your feebleness, but accept your strengths, as well. Once you start being honest with yourself, it's easy to get so caught up in pinpointing failures that you forget to see the strengths in your life, too—such as the talents God has entrusted to you and, most importantly, the grace He has provided to cover over all your failures.

## Investing in the Unveiled You

It's interesting to notice what people invest in, especially because investments reveal our priorities in life, whether we realize it or not. Some invest in stocks and bonds, others invest in jewelry, while still others invest in cars. Investments don't have to be material, either. People can invest in their families, their careers, their pastimes, and even their pets. Whatever the investment, however, one truth remains: Investments are those things in life that we give our attention to. They are the undertakings, interests, and items that consume our time, money, and thoughts. Whether we realize it or not, we are all making investments every day.

> What we invest in reveals our priorities in life, whether we realize it or not.

It's important that we conscientiously *choose* our investments. Some investments are tragic. For example, I have seen men and women invest five, ten, or even twenty years into non-marriage relationships, only to have those relationships ultimately end in disaster. Are you making wise investments? Or are you putting your time, energy, thoughts, and money into things that will inevitably crumble?

Ultimately, as Jesus taught us, we should be investing in eternal things—things that are not of this world but rather of the world to come:

*Do not lay up for yourselves treasures on earth, where moth and rust destroy and where thieves break in and steal; but lay up for yourselves treasures in heaven, where neither moth nor rust destroys and where thieves do not break in and steal.* (Matthew 6:19–20)

But even if we're already making eternal investments, we will still find ourselves having to make day-to-day decisions about more temporal investments. Which car should I put my money into? Which weekend chore should I devote my energy to? Which book or magazine should I read to fill these few spare moments? These may be temporal investments, since they do not determine our eternal destination as our decision to accept Christ does, but these decisions are by no means trivial. Every decision that we make has long-term consequences, and we do well to carefully consider our investments before we make them.

> Many people fail to make wise investments because they do not know what to invest in.

Most people don't neglect to make wise investments on purpose. They just don't have enough information to know what to invest in. It's rather like the need for taking vitamins. While most people realize the need to take some type of supplemental vitamin for their body to function optimally on a daily basis, many don't know where to start. Do I start with vitamin A, vitamin C, vitamin B complex, or all of the above? Should I take minerals? What about magnesium? Without enough information, it's difficult to make an informed decision about which vitamins to invest in.

Often, when we don't have enough information, we feel embarrassed. Rather than go public with our ignorance, we withdraw from others, and the result is physical, spiritual, emotional, and intellectual apathy in our lives. While this may be the easy route—much like putting on a mask—it isn't the route we should take, for it ultimately leaves us shaky and unstable. Are you ready to make the investments you need to make? Are you prepared to seek after the information that's necessary for such investments?

In the next section of this book, I would like to show you how to start making investments into your own life, investments that will yield great dividends for the future. Realize that as you make investments into yourself—into your health, your emotions, your mind, and your spirit—you are building a most important foundation, the one within you. Building this solid foundation will bring rewards for years to come, for it is through this foundation that God is able to effect change and growth in your life.

## Chapter Six

# F.O.U.N.D.A.T.I.O.N.—
# An Acrostic

A n acrostic is an arrangement of words in which certain letters in each word spell out another word when taken in order. One of the interesting things about acrostics is that the "building block" words help to define and explain the main word that they comprise. In many ways, acrostics help explain words and clarify their nuances.

I have taken the time here to suggest a word for each letter in *foundation*. Each word represents what I believe to be an essential element of a solid foundation. Keep these elements in mind as you continue working through this book, and as you establish solid foundations in your own life. It is only through employing each of these elements and the concepts they represent that you can fully strengthen your church, marriage, or business.

This is not an exhaustive list. There are many other elements that help make up a solid foundation, elements that the following chapters of this book will address and discuss in depth. Perhaps by the book's end, you may even want to make your own acrostic for *foundation*, with new words standing for each letter. However, I hope the acrostic provided here increases your appreciation for and grasp of a solid foundation as it lays the groundwork for the chapters to come.

F—Friends
O—Other-centeredness
U—Understanding
N—Needs
D—Direction
A—Attentiveness
T—Teachability
I—Intentionality
O—Operation
N—Naturalness

# Friends

*Friendships* are crucial for any foundation. God has created us as social beings and we deeply crave and require relationships of all levels in order to function properly on a day-to-day basis. As the nineteenth-century author Henry van Dyke once said, "A friend is what the heart needs all the time." [1]

Unfortunately, the word *friend* is quite recklessly used and misused. Anybody can claim to be your friend, even if they have only met you once. Some people make false claims of being friends with a superstar celebrity, even though they have never actually spoken with that person.

---

1. Quotes and Sayings Database. <http://www.quotesandsayings.com/gpromise.htm> (9 April, 2003)

And oftentimes people will claim to be a person's friend just because that person has a great deal of money, influence, or fame. As Proverbs says, *"Wealth makes many friends, but the poor is separated from his friend....Many entreat the favor of the nobility, and every man is a friend to one who gives gifts"* (Proverbs 19:4, 6). Is this really friendship?

Merriam-Webster defines *friend* as "one attached to another by affection or esteem; acquaintance." [2] As this definition suggests, a friend is someone you are acquainted with. But true friendship goes far beyond mere acquaintance. It requires self-sacrifice and wholehearted, unconditional love. One of the best explanations I have ever seen concerning friendship is recorded

> Our greatest example of how to be a friend is Jesus Christ.

in the book of Proverbs, which was written by Solomon, the wisest man who ever lived: *"A man who has friends must himself be friendly, but there is a friend who sticks closer than a brother"* (Proverbs 18:24).

We can find many examples of close friendship in Scripture, from the friendship between David and Jonathan to the friendship between Ruth and Naomi. (See 1 Samuel 18:1–4; 20:1–42; Ruth 1:1–18.) Ultimately our greatest example of how to be a friend is found in Jesus Christ, for He referred to those who belong to Him as friends: *"You are My friends if you do whatever I command you. No longer do I call you servants, for a servant does not know what his master is doing; but I have called you friends, for all things that I heard from My Father I have made known to you"* (John 15:14–15). We should treat others with the same love, patience, and self-sacrifice that Christ shows to us.

2. *Merriam-Webster's Collegiate Dictionary,* Electronic Edition, Version 1.1, s.v. "friend."

A friend is someone who will be there through hard times. As John Churton Collins, a nineteenth-century literary critic once said, "In prosperity, our friends know us; in adversity, we know our friends." [3] I've always believed that you cannot really determine who your real friends are until you get into some sort of trouble. It is a blessing when the Lord provides us with friends who are devoted like this. There are some people in my life that I know, beyond a doubt, would be there if I ever needed them, even though I may not talk to them every day.

Only when everyone else has turned against you or maligned your name will you discover who your real friends are. Real friends always respond affirmatively in the midst of your negative situations. Friends will help you when you're down. True friends do not only see where you are now but also where you will be in the future. Their mere presence helps catapult you toward victory.

My dearest personal friend, Dr. Michael Graves, has been my friend for more than thirty-eight years now. He is now the pastor at Temple Baptist Church in Nashville, Tennessee, but we met back during my early years at American Baptist College. To be quite honest, Michael didn't like me at all back then. He thought I was arrogant. In my second year of college, however, those walls came down. Michael and I started having dinner together, studying together, and communicating with each other more openly. He taught me some valuable lessons that I cherish to this day, such as the art of comprehension and the value of sharing.

Throughout the many years that have followed, Michael and I have shared in much meaningful dialogue and fellowship. In a lot of ways, I believe some of the success

3. Famous People's Quotes. <http://www.olympicpc.com/quotes/collins_john_churton.html> (9 April, 2003)

within both of our ministries can be linked to our friend-ship. As the book of Proverbs says, we have helped "sharpen" each other's spirits: *"As iron sharpens iron, so a man sharpens the countenance of his friend"* (Proverbs 27:17).

Not all friendships are as intimate as this, though. We can have friendships with the people we interact with every day—our coworkers, our neighbors, our church family. Friendship does not always mean having barbe-cues together, going fishing together, or seeing movies at the theater together. There are levels of friendship, and some are more casual than others. In fact, it's not just that we *can* have relationships at many levels but that we *should.* A pastor should be a friend to his church, a father should be a friend to his children, and a business execu-tive should be a friend to his employees. While people in such positions should be more than just friends—a father must discipline his children, for example, which may not seem so friendly—an element of friendship is essential for success. To put it plainly, friendship is foundational to any foundation.

# Other-centeredness

James 1:19 advises us to be *"swift to hear, slow to speak, slow to wrath."* Perhaps that is why God gave us two ears and only one mouth. Maybe He intends for us to listen twice as much as we speak. Think how many conflicts and misunderstandings would be avoided if we would only be more cautious about what we said and more eager to hear what others had to say.

Clearly God desires us to put others first. He longs for us to be what I like to call *other-centered.* This is founda-tional to any undertaking in life. Unfortunately, our society is wired quite the opposite. The "me" emphasis of the '80s seems to be as alive as ever, and putting others first seems like the last thing anyone wants to do.

Perhaps you've seen this in the business world. Many businessmen eagerly solicit our patronage and support, realizing that it is essential for the existence of their businesses. Initially, such businesspeople seem to have a genuine interest in meeting our needs and helping us. This spirit of service, however, quickly fades once a little bit of money has been transferred from our hands to theirs. Now, I'm not saying that all business interactions are like this, but it certainly isn't uncommon. Such behavior does not suggest genuine concern but rather a focus on a person's money instead of the person himself.

> People, from the oldest to the youngest, want to know that they count.

Sadly, this self-centered mentality can even be spotted in the health industry today. Consider the recent movie *John Q*, starring Denzel Washington. This film depicts a side of our health care system that many people would rather ignore. Washington portrayed a father who was denied health care for his dying child and felt forced to take matters into his own hands. As unfortunate as it is, it's true that those without proper funds often do not receive quality health care. As the old saying goes, "You get what you pay for." Especially in regard to life-and-death cases, it would seem that the preservation of human life would take precedence over money, but often this is not the case. Many people have been made to feel like mere numbers in a cold, impersonal system. Whoever has the most wealth connected to their number gets royal treatment, while those who lack financial strength are often overlooked and slighted.

People, from the oldest to the youngest, want to know that they count. They want to know that people care and have a genuine interest in them, not just in what they have to offer. It is crucial that we put others first and show genuine concern. Remember the Golden Rule? *"Therefore, whatever you want men to do to you, do also to them, for this is the Law and the Prophets"* (Matthew 7:12). Nobody wants to feel "used" in friendships, business interactions, or any other kind of relationship. We all desire to be valued as the people God has made us to be. As Christians, we must take extra steps to ensure that others feel valued over and above ourselves.

# Understanding

Just as we can exhibit humility through other-centered actions, we can practice humility in our quest for *understanding.* Consider Proverbs 4:7. It reads, *"Wisdom is the principal thing; therefore get wisdom. And in all your getting, get understanding."* Understanding is critical for the building of any foundation.

One of the difficult realities in life revolves around the fact that we always want to be heard and understood. This is part of our nature, and although there's nothing intrinsically wrong with this desire, an overemphasis on it can lead to a lot of conflict and struggle.

At the heart of good relationship and communication skills lies the ability not only to hear what others are saying but also to understand it. There's a world of difference between mere hearing and actual understanding. Hearing is a physical act of the ears, while understanding is an intellectual and emotional act of the mind and heart.

> Seek first to understand, then to be understood.

Understanding takes humility. It requires you to take time to carefully consider the information that is being presented to you. It also requires that you try to understand before you try to be understood. This is crucial for the foundation of anything we undertake. Seek first to understand, then to be understood.

This rule definitely applies to marriage. When one spouse impatiently insists on being heard, the other may respond by shutting down. When both spouses sincerely desire to hear and understand each other, however, the groundwork for trust and healthy communication has been laid.

Understanding is important to marriage in another way, as well. When Proverbs 4:7 tells us to, *"get understanding,"* it means that we must gather all the information we can *before* we make a decision. Before two people enter into marriage, both need a complete understanding of their own characters, as well as the character of their intended. Never marry someone before you have assessed their greatest needs. I have seen the disaster that results when people marry for their new spouse's looks, smile, or charm. Although such characteristics should have some place in the decision to marry, they should never be the focus of a godly man searching for his wife. Every man needs to first understand his woman's needs. It is the man who will have to fill most of those needs throughout the lifetime of the marriage. Knowing beforehand whether or not he's willing and able to handle this responsibility could save a lot of heartache in the end.

Getting understanding applies to other areas of life, as well. Before starting a business, for instance, you should get an understanding of the needs of your potential market. Test your market. See if your service will be one that is useful in that area. For instance, the snow shovel that sells so well in Michigan, probably won't do so well in Florida. Perhaps your product is more suitable for another part of the country.

This is a very fundamental principle, one which, when correctly understood, can prevent a lot of unnecessary headaches and heartaches. Jesus described it like this:

*For which of you, intending to build a tower, does not sit down first and count the cost, whether he has enough to finish it; lest, after he has laid the foundation, and is not able to finish, all who see it begin to mock him, saying, "This man began to build and was not able to finish."* (Luke 14:28–30)

Before we start laying any foundation, we must first get understanding. Count the cost before you start breaking ground.

# Needs

Why do we worry? Usually it's because we're fearful that a certain need won't be met. We won't be able to finish the project that's due at work next week. Or we can't snag the loan we need to start our church's new building project. Or maybe we're fearful that we won't get the necessary immune system boost to successfully recover from the surgery we're about to undergo. And so we worry.

But what does the Lord teach us about worrying? In this famous passage from Jesus' Sermon on the Mount, Jesus showed how we should respond (or not respond) to worry.

*Therefore I say to you, do not worry about your life, what you will eat or what you will drink; nor about your body, what you will put on. Is not life more than food and the body more than clothing? Look at the birds of the air, for they neither sow nor reap nor gather into barns; yet your heavenly*

*Father feeds them. Are you not of more value than they? Which of you by worrying can add one cubit to his stature? So why do you worry about clothing? Consider the lilies of the field, how they grow: they neither toil nor spin; and yet I say to you that even Solomon in all his glory was not arrayed like one of these. Now if God so clothes the grass of the field, which today is, and tomorrow is thrown into the oven, will He not much more clothe you, O you of little faith? Therefore do not worry, saying, "What shall we eat?" or "What shall we drink?" or "What shall we wear?" For after all these things the Gentiles seek. For your heavenly Father knows that you need all these things. But seek first the kingdom of God and His righteousness, and all these things shall be added to you. Therefore do not worry about tomorrow, for tomorrow will worry about its own things. Sufficient for the day is its own trouble.*
(Matthew 6:25–34)

As we learn from these verses, God is the supplier of all our *needs*. We have no cause to worry! This is essential in the building of any foundation.

One of the mistakes we often make is to rely on our flesh when we want to make things happen. Concerning this pitfall, the Bible gives the vivid example of Abraham and his wife Sarah, to whom God had promised a son despite their old age.

When God promises us something, it's already available; we simply need to appropriate it. But Abraham had his doubts, and so he tried to help God by having sexual relations, at Sarah's suggestion, with her Egyptian servant, Hagar. After all, Abraham reasoned, he was only making

God look good. If he didn't take matters into his own hands, God would end up looking foolish, right? Well, Hagar bore Abraham a son, Ishmael, but God did not honor Ishmael as the heir of faith since he was not born according to God's plan.

I suppose that it's human nature for us to try and help God out, but God despises the idea that we would ever discount His ability to provide for His creation. No matter what our needs are, God is our Supplier. Sometimes we divide things into categories of what we believe God can do or will do and what He can't or won't. Such categorization is wrong, for He is able to supply our every need.

Even though God is able to supply all our needs, He may not always choose to. Why? Because He sees things from a different perspective than we do. He sees needs in our lives that must be attended to more than the needs we are praying for. Sometimes we need to be deprived of one thing that we think we need simply

> No matter what our needs are, God is our Supplier.

so God can satisfy a greater, deeper need in our lives. God supplies our needs according to His riches, not ours. That alone should bring great encouragement. His supply is not based on anything about us, but solely upon His eternal worth.

Whatever your need may be—whether it is physical, emotional, mental, financial, or spiritual—God is your Source. Please realize this before you start anything. Recognize this truth before you get married, start a business, or build a church. People come and people go, but God is always faithful and ever constant. As Isaiah 2:22 says, *"Stop trusting in man, who has but a breath in his nostrils. Of what account is he?"* (NIV). While we cannot be confident in the provisions of any man or institution, we can always depend upon our God. *"And my God shall supply all your need according to His riches in glory by Christ Jesus"* (Philippians 4:19).

# Direction

Another thing that is essential to a solid foundation is divine *direction.* We must seek and follow the Lord's leading and guidance in our lives if we want to have confidence in the foundation we are laying.

Over the years I have had people ask me, "Pastor, how will I know that I'm being led by the Lord and not by the enemy?" Although most of the people who ask this question are sincere Christians who simply want to make sure they are walking in obedience, their question shows that they have misunderstood a key element in their salvation. As sons and daughters of God, we can be confident that His Spirit will lead us, not the devil or his evil spirits. *"For as many as are led by the Spirit of God, these are sons of God"* (Romans 8:14). Being led by the Spirit is the mark of a believer.

The fact of the matter is that God leads all His children. Whether or not we choose to follow Him is a different topic, but the truth remains that He never fails to lead those whom He calls His own. Even when we feel alone in times of darkness, trial, and temptation, God is still leading us. *"Yea, though I walk through the valley of the shadow of death, I will fear no evil; for You are with me; Your rod and Your staff, they comfort me"* (Psalm 23:4).

When we follow God's direction, we can't get lost. Certainly there will be times of testing and wilderness experiences when it seems that God has totally forgotten us. But we must not despair, for the Lord never forgets or leaves us. *"He Himself has said, 'I will never leave you nor forsake you'"* (Hebrews 13:5). The wilderness experiences you pass through have purpose, and that is to develop your character. God tests you to see whether or not you qualify for the blessings that are in store.

As long as you follow the Lord's leading, you're walking in safety. It is only when you begin to heed the enemy's voice and promptings that you will see everything that you have worked so long and so hard for start to crumble. Stay on the Lord's path. Fortunately, our Lord is patient. Even when we do start to stray, He will gently guide us back onto the right pathway. *"Whether you turn to the right or to the left, your ears will hear a voice behind you, saying, 'This is the way; walk in it'"* (Isaiah 30:21 NIV).

# Attentiveness and Teachability

The ability to be *attentive* and the willingness to be *teachable* are fundamental to a solid foundation. As the book of Proverbs admonishes us, we should be eager to grow as well as ready to take the steps necessary to do so.

*"Hear, my children, the instruction of a father, and give attention to know understanding"* (Proverbs 4:1).

Sons can save themselves a lot of time and trouble if they will only heed the instruction of their fathers. My spiritual father, to whom I owe much, is the Rev. L. A. Hamblin. I believe that I learned more from watching his life than I did from anything else.

Although I asked pertinent questions when necessary, I always paid close attention to the way he lived his life and to how he did things. As a consequence, although Rev. Hamblin was an exceptional preacher, teacher, and pastor, he did not have to preach for me to get the message, for his life was a sermon. Because I admired the man so greatly, I studied his life, taking careful note of his methods. I still use some of those methods in my work today.

You see, a father's instruction does not always have to be verbal. Oftentimes it is by example. In fact, example usually trumps verbal instruction when it comes to learning lessons. Why else do people find it necessary to say, "Do as I say, not as I do"? Parents use this with their children when they know their actions set a bad example. They know the fundamental truth that actions always speak louder than words, so they find it necessary to remind their children not to imitate everything they do.

> Good things do not just happen. You must plan to bring them about.

This is an important truth for us to grasp as we're laying our solid foundation, for if we choose to be attentive to the good examples set by those around us, we are sure to grow. It is only when we pay attention and cultivate an attitude that's teachable, however, that we will understand the message. A teachable spirit is necessary if we are to succeed in any area of life. God cannot do anything with a person who has a proud and haughty spirit. Know-it-alls, in fact, actually know very little, primarily because they refuse to let new information enter their lives.

Even though the Lord has allowed me to lead a great ministry for more than three decades now, I still seek opportunities to learn from others. I choose to be teachable. As long as I am teachable, God can use me to do far greater things than what has already been done. However, once I start believing that I know all there is to know about the spiritual life, soul-winning, church-building, pastoring, or simply being a leader, then I will fail miserably.

This message takes on new significance when we consider the changing nature of the world we live in today. Things are rapidly changing in our modern world. In order for me, as a pastor, to remain relevant to the people of this modern era, I must change. That change can only come as I am attentive to the changes themselves and teachable enough to accept them.

For the person desiring to lay and maintain a solid foundation, attentiveness and teachability are crucial. Those who opt for inattentiveness and an unteachable spirit set themselves up for failure and defeat: *"Pride goes before destruction, and a haughty spirit before a fall"* (Proverbs 16:18). Those who remain attentive and teachable, however, will reap great reward in God's kingdom, both now and in the life to come.

# Intentionality and Operation

In order to lay a solid foundation in your life, you must be *intentional* about pursuing it. Good things do not just happen. You must plan, or strategize, and then implement those plans and strategies to bring good things about.

Consider, for instance, this verse from Nehemiah, which talks about rebuilding the walls of Jerusalem after their destruction during the Babylonian captivity: *"So we built the wall, and the entire wall was joined together up to half its height, for the people had a mind to work"* (Nehemiah 4:6). Were the Israelites ho-hum, half-hearted, and haphazard about building this wall? No! They *"had a mind to work."* In other words, they knew their goal and they did everything in their power to move toward it. This is what it means to be intentional.

However, the Israelites were not just intentional. They followed up this intentionality with actual *operation*, or action, in order to achieve the task at hand. This, too, is critical for laying any foundation in your life. If you merely "have a mind to work" but do not take actions to actually build the wall, you will get nowhere.

The Lord promises to bless the work of your hands, and He will always do more than you ever expect Him to do. However, you need to get those hands moving before He cant start blessing them. When you take action, it shows God that you are serious about going forward and progressing. He guarantees that He will bless and prosper the works of your hands, but you must first produce something to bless!

What would you do if you knew that everything your hands touched would turn to gold? My guess is that you would be touching a lot of stuff! Well, God has promised to turn to spiritual gold everything that we patiently and persistently pursue for the furthering of His kingdom. *"The LORD your God will bless you in all your produce and in all the work of your hands, so that you surely rejoice"* (Deuteronomy 16:15). Are you being intentional and then taking actions to see those intentions through to completion?

# Naturalness

In order to lay a solid foundation in your life, you need to be *natural*. By this I mean that you must be original, or genuine. You must strive toward those things that God has fashioned and created you to do.

You see, God has made you unique. You are unlike any other person. If He didn't create you from a carbon copy of someone else, then why should you make your goals and plans carbon copies of others' goals and plans?

Often this can be challenging, especially when the purposes He's created us for and the plans He's calling us toward seem impossible to attain. But remember, nothing is impossible with God. The plans he has set for you may be altogether new and untested, something that you've never seen done in anyone else's life. God will bring these plans to pass, though, according to His perfect will and in His perfect timing.

No matter what He's called you to, you can be certain of one thing: He's also called you to lay a solid foundation as you're working toward that aim. It is only then—when you are seeking the help of *friends*, striving to be *other-centered*, reaching for better *understanding*, recognizing God as the fulfiller of your *needs*, following His *direction*, exercising *attentiveness*, showing a spirit of *teachability*, facing your goals with *intentionality*, and fulfilling those goals through *operation*—that God will bless the foundation of your unique and *natural* life.

# Part II

## Preparing Yourself for Success

# Chapter Seven
# Caring for Your Body

H ere in America, we are a very appearance-conscious people. Just think about all the magazine, billboard, and Internet ads you see every day for cosmetics, anti-wrinkle creams, diet pills, and exercise equipment. Every year, Americans spend billions of dollars on health and beauty products in an attempt to look, think, and feel younger. According to the U.S. Census Bureau, health and personal care stores in the United States averaged $184,153 *million* in the year 2002 alone! [1] Whether these natural (or not-so-natural) cures really work differs from one formula to the next, but one truth remains: People want to stay young, no matter what the cost.

Ironically, while our culture is so concerned with staying fit, trim, and young, many of us abuse our bodies daily. We don't give our bodies the exercise they need, we sleep less than we should, we eat more dessert than is good for us, and

---

1. "Time Series Data Monthly Retail Sales & Seasonal Factors, 1992–2003." U.S. Census Bureau. <http://www.census.gov/svsd/www/adseries.html> (4 April, 2003)

we continue to neglect the vitamins and healthful foods that we know will benefit our bodies. Now, before you say to me, "Pastor Bailey, this body is temporary. The Lord's giving me a new one when He returns, so I don't have to worry about this one," let me remind you of a Bible verse that I'm sure you know.

> *Or do you not know that your body is the temple of the Holy Spirit who is in you, whom you have from God, and you are not your own? For you were bought at a price; therefore glorify God **in your body** and in your spirit, which are God's.*
> (1 Corinthians 6:19–20, emphasis added)

Now, I'm not a health crusader, trying to preach an herbal salvation. There's no verse in the Bible that says we're required to try this anti-wrinkle cream, that diet pill, those exercise machines, and these new vitamin supplements. However, God's Word is very clear that we *are* supposed to care for the bodies He has entrusted to us.

In this chapter, we'll look at some basics principles we must follow if we want to care for our bodies. In other words, we'll investigate how each of us can lay a solid foundation in the physical realm of our lives.

## Our Bodies Are the Temple of God

The apostle Paul reminded the Corinthian believers that their physical bodies were *"temple*[s] *of the Holy Spirit"* (v. 19). God dwelt in them, and the same is true for believers today. But God does not simply dwell in our temple-bodies; He *owns* them. God is not a squatter, someone who starts building on land before it's legally his. Instead, God is our Owner, for He has paid a very high price for us with the blood of His Son. Our lives—including our bodies—are not are own. They are God's property.

If you have ever leased or rented a property to live in, you probably received a list of restrictions concerning that property. These may have included "no pets," "no painting the walls," or "no hanging pictures that will leave holes in the walls." Perhaps, in addition to this list of "don'ts," there was even a list of things you were expected to do—take care of the lawn, keep the house or apartment fairly clean, and pay all utility bills while living in the property. Often, the property owner will even require you to leave a security deposit, just in case you don't abide by the rules. Understandably, it's important to the landowner that you take care of his possession. While you live on his property, you are expected to keep it in a condition that is pleasing to him.

Our bodies are the same. Think of your body as "leased property." You are leasing your body from God, the Owner, and you have an agreement with Him to take care of His property. Any decisions to alter, add on, or remodel His property have to be cleared by the Landlord first.

> Think of your body as "leased property."

## Our Bodies Are Meant to Serve Others

In this earthly realm, you'll need your body for whatever tasks God has called you to accomplish, so don't abuse or neglect it. Imagine if you neglected to change your car's oil for a whole year. What would happen? The engine would probably quit working. In the same manner, imagine what would happen to your body if you didn't take proper "maintenance steps" by exercising, eating good foods, and getting plenty of sleep. Getting from point A to point B would suddenly become very difficult.

It is important for us to keep our bodies as highly functional as we can, and this means taking care of our "engines." I don't claim to be a health professional who can prescribe a specific diet and exercise routine that's just right for you, but I do claim to be a pastor who has seen amazing benefits in his own life from simply making healthy decisions. I use a treadmill every day, lift weights for strength training two to three times a week, and try to make healthy decisions about what I eat. My main reason for doing these things is that I realize what I'm worth to my family, my congregation, my community, and, most importantly, my God. If my body were rendered useless because of neglect, then I could no longer give my best to the God whom I love so much.

There are many gifted and talented people who are now forced to live in convalescent homes, hospitals, or rehabilitation centers, and many others who are hindered from giving their best, simply because they made unhealthy decisions. I'm saddened when I see such greatly gifted people unable to serve God to the fullest, simply because they chose to ignore their bodies' calls for help. I'm even more disturbed when I see young pastors and spiritual leaders grow ill, or even die, far too early in life because of exhaustion, hypertension, and other maladies brought on by neglect of the body. Many of these deaths could have been prevented if these people had simply invested a little time into caring for their bodies.

## Making a Meaningful Commitment

As with many good intentions in life, we often make commitments to improve our health but then quickly fail to carry it out because of forgetfulness, busyness, lack of motivation, or whatever. Writing our commitments down on paper, however, has an amazing way of making them "stick." When we write things down, we take them more seriously, we remember them more easily, and we have something to refer to as a motivator whenever we don't feel like sticking to the commitment.

Writing also helps us to be more specific about our goals. "Be healthier" is a noble goal, but it's not very easy to implement. Where do you start? What's the first step toward "being healthier"? Writing things down lets you map out a plan. When you write things down, you can get as detailed as necessary without having to worry about forgetting all the fine points.

For instance, if your goal is "be healthier," write down specifics on how you'll accomplish that goal. Will you replace your afternoon snack of a candy bar and soda with a piece of fruit and glass of milk instead? Will you go to bed earlier each night so that you are more rested each day? Will you start walking, jogging, or running around your neighborhood every day? Be specific and write it down. Then, check in on yourself every so often. Return to that little piece of paper with your detailed plan to see how well you're holding up. If you've deviated from it, don't despair. Just focus on getting back on track for the next week. Pretty soon, you'll find that little piece of paper to be an accountability partner and motivator in one.

Whatever your plan for being healthier is, it's important that you target three key areas. First, exercise is essential. Write down an exercise plan that you can stick to. Be sure that it includes some form of cardiovascular activity (something that gets your heart and lungs working) for at least 20 minutes, 3 days a week. You can even write down several exercise options and bounce back and forth between them so you don't get bored. Try running, walking, aerobics, TaeBo, dancing, swimming, or anything else that gets your heart pumping faster and your lungs working harder. If you'd like, list your new exercise plan here, or record it in your own separate journal. If you choose to use this page for your exercise plan, fill in the "exercise" blank with the type of exercise you will engage in. Under "frequency," state how many times per week you will perform this activity. And under "length," record the amount of time in minutes that you will perform the exercise each time you do it.

Exercise _____ Frequency _____ Length _____

Exercise _____ Frequency _____ Length _____

Exercise _____ Frequency _____ Length _____

The second key area that must be targeted in a health-improvement plan is that of diet. Once again, I'm no expert when it comes to figuring out what foods we should eat. I'm not a dietitian, but I do know some basic principles—principles that you're probably aware of, too, in our health-conscious culture. If you'd like more guidelines on deciding which types and amounts of food should be included in your diet, I encourage you to read more about it. You might want to start with *What Would Jesus Eat?*, *Walking in Divine Health*, or *Toxic Relief*, all written by Dr. Don Colbert.

After you have evaluated what you currently eat and compared it to what you *should* be eating, I encourage you to write down a meal plan. It can be as detailed as you like or as sketchy as you like, but write it down. I suggest starting off with two simple lists: "Foods to Avoid" and "Foods to Include." On the "Foods to Avoid" list, put down those foods which aren't necessarily the best for you, but that you eat pretty often. Gradually work through the list, limiting the amount you eat of each food. On the "Foods to Include" list, put down those foods which *are* good for you, but that you have not been getting enough of. Gradually work through this list, too, progressively including more and more of these healthful foods into your diet. Here's a chart to get you started:

Foods to Avoid:           Foods to Include:

1. _____     1. _____

2. _____     2. _____

3. _____     3. _____

4. _____     4. _____

5. _____     5. _____

6. _____     6. _____

The third and final key issue to target as you work toward a healthier lifestyle is the amount of sleep you get each night. Sleep is crucial for healthy living. Without it, we put ourselves at risk for all kinds of medical problems because our immune systems are weakened whenever we don't get enough sleep. Additionally, our alertness, concentration level, and ability to remember things throughout the day decreases significantly if we don't get enough sleep. You probably know this just from personal experience.

The average American does not get nearly enough sleep. Most health professionals recommend that we get somewhere between seven and nine hours of uninterrupted sleep each night. Unfortunately, many people's sleep intake falls far below this range.

Perhaps you feel that such a goal is more dream than obtainable reality. Most people are just too busy to slow down and rest. But getting more sleep at night really is worth it, even if it means having to cut back on some of your activities and commitments during the day. As you allow yourself to get more sleep, you might even find your energy and productivity levels increasing—meaning you'll be able to accomplish your daily tasks with more speed and efficiency than before, ultimately freeing yourself up for even more time to rest.

Sometimes I come across people who think that getting by on very little sleep is a sign of strength. Some of them are Christians who seem to hold the attitude that not getting enough sleep is somehow super-spiritual. I think these people equate busyness for God's kingdom with holiness and obedience. Sometimes they even go so far as to hold the attitude that sleep and rest are somehow self-indulgent and displeasing to God. Have you seen attitudes and thought processes like this before? Perhaps, if you think about it, you'll even spot it in your own life. But the truth of the matter is, God has commanded us to rest.

> God designed our bodies to need rest and instructed us to do so.

*Remember the Sabbath day, to keep it holy. Six days you shall labor and do all your work, but the seventh day is the Sabbath of the LORD your God. In it you shall do no work: you, nor your son, nor your daughter, nor your male servant, nor your female servant, nor your cattle, nor your stranger who is within your gates. For in six days the LORD made the heavens and the earth, the sea, and all that is in them, and rested the seventh day. Therefore the LORD blessed the Sabbath day and hallowed it.* (Exodus 20:8–11)

We can be confident that God desires us to rest, for He has designed our bodies to need rest and He has instructed us to do so, even if that means taking a nap during the day. Taking time out of our busy days to replenish our body's energy is by no means self-indulgent or sinful. The sooner we realize this, the sooner many Christians will stop burning themselves out through years of hard work without rest.

In my own life, I have made it a practice to rest whenever my body is feeling fatigued. Our bodies will always tell us what they need, but are we listening?

Now, if you know you're not getting the sleep that your body needs, record your resolution to get more sleep here:

I will sleep at least _____ hours each night. I will go to bed at an early enough hour each evening to ensure that I get the amount of sleep that I need to be in peak condition the next day. As time permits, I will occasionally take naps to recharge my body. Since my body is God's temple, I will not put unnecessary wear and tear on it by depriving myself of rest. I am fully aware that God has given me only one body, so I choose to keep it in the best possible shape.

_____
Signed

These small changes in your exercise, diet, and sleep schedule may not seem important at the moment, but I guarantee that they will make a world of difference in the long run. As you take these small steps and continue implementing healthy decisions, you will be well on your way to building a solid foundation for healthiness in your life.

# Chapter Eight
# Nurturing Your Soul

he concept of the soul can be confusing, especially since the word *soul* is often used interchangeably with the word *spirit*. I certainly do not want to add to the confusion, but rather I hope to clarify for you what the soul is according to Scripture and to establish how we, as Christians, can invest in our souls' growth, as the Bible calls us to do.

The soul is essential to life. Without our souls, we would be dead. The soul is at the core of our being; it is what "runs" us, so to speak. Or, another way to understand it, the soul is our operating system.

An operating system is what allows a computer to do its work. As Merriam-Webster defines it, an *operating system* is "software that controls the operation of a computer and directs the processing of programs." [1] You're probably familiar with the specific names of operating systems, such as Microsoft Windows, Apple Mac OS, or Linux, to name a few. Without one of these programs, your computer would

---

1. *Merriam-Webster's Collegiate Dictionary*, Electronic Edition, Version 1.1, s.v. "operating system."

be little more than a heap of plastic and electronic circuitry. Until the operating system has been installed, you can't run any software. An operating system gives life to the computer, making it workable. In similar fashion, our souls are what animate us, allowing us to function and work properly. Without our God-breathed souls, we would be much like a computer with no operating system installed.

Scholars have credited the soul with functions of thinking and willing, and often speak of it interchangeably with the mind. Since it is in the soul that thought takes place and the will is exercised, it is here that the ability to choose and make decisions resides.

The great church father St. Augustine described the soul in this way:

> It is even our rational faculty, whereby the soul exercises sense and intelligence,—not, indeed, the sensation which is felt by the bodily senses, but the operation of that innermost sense from which arises the term sentiment. Owing to this it is, no doubt, that we are placed above brute animals, since these are unendowed with reason. [2]

Our abilities to think, reason, and make willful choices all arise from the soul—which, as St. Augustine pointed out, separate us from animals. Since the soul is the powerhouse of our existence and home to our thoughts, reasoning, and decision-making capability, shouldn't we take time to invest in its health and well-being? The first step in this process is eliminating those things that are harmful to the soul.

---

2. St. Aurelius Augustine, "Wide and Narrow Sense of the Word 'Spirit,'" *On the Soul and Its Origins,* Book IV, Chapter 37. Accessed at <http://www.ccel.org.> (9 April, 2003)

## Guard the Entry Gate to the Soul

There's a Sunday school song—maybe you know it— called "Be Careful, Little Eyes." It goes something like this:

> Be careful, little eyes, what you see.
> Be careful, little eyes, what you see.
> There's a Father up above,
> Looking down in tender love,
> So, be careful, little eyes, what you see. [3]

The song then continues through several different body parts—"Be careful, little ears, what you hear," "Be careful, little mouth, what you say," and "Be careful, little feet, where you go," to name just a few. The point of the song is to remind children to avoid those things that could contaminate their souls. As Christians, no matter what our age, we are to guard our souls by keeping out thoughts, words, images, and ideas that compromise our ability to think, reason, and make decisions in a godly fashion.

You've probably heard the expression "garbage in, garbage out." To return to the computer analogy, technology gurus remember this principle whenever they write computer programs. If they enter incorrect or incomplete data, their results will be incorrect or incomplete, as well. The output will only be as good as the information that's inputted. The same holds true for our souls. If we put garbage in, we're sure to get garbage out.

During His time on earth, Jesus referred to this principle. In response to a group of Pharisees who were challenging Him, He said, *"Brood of vipers! How can you, being evil, speak good things? For out of the abundance of the heart the mouth speaks"* (Matthew 12:34). In other words, our

---

3. Source: <http://www.ebibleteacher.com/children/songs.htm> (16 April, 2003)

actions arise from the overflow of our souls. The more we allow sinful thoughts, ideas, images, and words to enter our thoughts, the more that sinful thoughts, actions, and words will flow from our lives. As Christians, we are called to invest in our souls by conscientiously guarding what enters them. Take stock of your life right now. Are you allowing things to enter your soul that later manifest themselves as garbage in your life?

## You Are What You Think

Closely related to the "garbage in, garbage out" principle is this next principle for the soul: You are what you think. Remember what Jesus said?

> *Your dominant thoughts will manifest themselves in your life.*

*"For out of the abundance of the heart the mouth speaks"* (Matthew 12:34). If we input our souls with garbage, our thoughts will dwell on garbage, and the output of our lives will be garbage. Conversely, if we only permit good things to pass through the gateways of our souls, our thoughts will dwell on such good things, and the output of our lives will be good things.

You are what you think. Your dominant thoughts eventually manifest themselves in your life. Are you thinking upon things that are going to please God once they are "outputted" in your life? Paul had important words for the church in Philippi regarding this topic. He wrote,

> *Finally, brethren, whatever things are true, whatever things are noble, whatever things are just, whatever things are pure, whatever things are lovely, whatever things are of good report, if there is any virtue and if there is anything praiseworthy; meditate on these things.* (Philippians 4:8)

Paul encouraged the Philippian believers to reflect on things that were true, noble, just, pure, lovely, of good report, virtuous, and praiseworthy. Are you thinking on such things in your life? The strength of your foundation greatly depends on what you deposit into your soul and into your mind.

Right before God allowed the children of Israel to enter the Promised Land, He said the following to His people through Joshua:

*This Book of the Law shall not depart from your mouth, but you shall meditate in it day and night, that you may observe to do according to all that is written in it. For then you will make your way prosperous, and then you will have good success.*
(Joshua 1:8)

Notice what this verse says: The difference between spiritual success and spiritual failure depends on what we choose to think about. Furthermore, this verse tells us precisely what we should be thinking about, for it instructs us to meditate on God's Word. *"This Book of the Law shall not depart from your mouth, but you shall meditate in it day and night."* When we meditate on the Word of God, then we know His ways and are able to translate such knowledge into obedience: *"that* [we] *may observe to do according to all that is written in it."*

> The difference between spiritual success and spiritual failure depends on what we think about.

The Word of God is by far the most important nourishment needed for the soul, for it is here that we are able to learn God's eternal principles for life. God's Word should always be at the center of our "soul-nourishment" plan.

## Investing in Your Talents

We also glorify God whenever we take time to invest in the talents, abilities, and gifts that He has woven into our souls. Has He gifted you with the ability to understand cars and how to fix them? Then invest in that talent; take time to nourish your soul by filling it with a deeper, more far-reaching understanding of cars and car repair. Do you enjoy singing? Then learn to love it even more by expanding your knowledge of vocal music and by practicing. As you invest in your talents, gifts, and abilities, you will glorify God, for He is the fashioner of your soul and He delights to see your soul grow in wisdom and understanding.

Exercising the mind is one major way we can show God that we appreciate the gifts of knowledge and life that He has freely given us. To never learn and to refuse to exercise His gifts only insults the Creator. Try your best to read and feed your soul with things that will help you be better at what you do.

## Seeking Godly Counsel

Once we undertake this project of feeding our souls things that will help us be better at what we do, we need to make sure that we are getting this "food" from good sources. Psalm 1:1–3 says,

*Blessed is the man who walks not in the counsel of the ungodly, nor stands in the path of sinners, nor sits in the seat of the scornful; but his delight is in the law of the LORD, and in His law he meditates day and night. He shall be like a tree planted by the rivers of water, that brings forth its fruit in its season, whose leaf also shall not wither; and whatever he does shall prosper.*

In this much beloved psalm, we see a description of a blessed man. What makes him blessed, according to the psalm? The fact that he heeds only godly advice. He has chosen to take instruction only from those who are godly and to ignore the advice of those who are ungodly. As children of the Lord, we must guard our souls from the advice of those who have no covenant with God.

Now, in areas of secular interest, it is often fine to get advice from unspiritual people. For example, if I want to have an automobile repaired, I don't necessarily look for a person with great spiritual insight and an in-depth knowledge of the Scriptures. I look for someone who specializes in repairing the kind of car I own. I deal with that person because he's an expert in his field, not because he goes to Sunday school and church every Sunday.

In areas that relate to the spiritual realm, however, I refuse to seek counsel from the ungodly. For example, I would always seek marriage counseling from Christian marriage counselors. Why? Because marriage is an institution created and sustained by God. The person who counsels me on marriage should be someone who is intimately acquainted with the Creator and Sustainer of my marriage. I would never want to get marriage advice from someone who didn't respect God or understand His ways. That's a recipe for disaster! Would you ask your friend—who's never opened the hood of a car in his life—to help you fix your car when it breaks down? Of course not. Similarly, why would you seek marriage advice from someone who does not understand how God intended marriage to work? Such a person is likely to give advice that would hasten the end of your marriage instead of saving it.

Sometimes believers seek help from financial consultants to get out of debt, and it's not uncommon for such counselors to suggest cutting back on tithes and offerings in an attempt to save money. Nonbelievers do not grasp the importance of tithing. To their thinking, such funds should be funneled toward paying off a credit card debt or making mortgage payments. They don't understand the need for obedience to God when it comes to tithing, no matter how dire financial straits are. In fact, many Christians have been blessed with financial prosperity *because* of their obedience to God in the area of tithing. God's blessings do not always come in the form of financial prosperity, but often they do. In the Old Testament, for instance, God promised the children of Israel that He would bless them materially if they were materially obedient to Him through tithing:

> *"Bring all the tithes into the storehouse, that there may be food in My house, and try Me now in this," says the LORD of hosts, "If I will not open for you the windows of heaven and pour out for you such blessing that there will not be room enough to receive it. And I will rebuke the devourer for your sakes, so that he will not destroy the fruit of your ground, nor shall the vine fail to bear fruit for you in the field," says the LORD of hosts.* (Malachi 3:10–11)

It doesn't make sense to non-believers to give away money with the expectation that all needs will still be taken care of. Like marriage, financial issues are something for which we should always seek godly, Bible-focused counsel.

## Making a Meaningful Commitment

Just as you made a written commitment to invest in the health of your body, you can make a commitment to feed and nourish your soul. Use the following as a guide.

I commit to reading and meditating on the Bible for at least _____ minutes each day so that my

soul is filled with godly principles for living obedi-
ently to my Lord. I will begin by reading the book of
_____.

I owe it to myself to read at least ____ books each
month, whether they be novels, biographies, or anything of interest to me. I commit to doing this now.

I will learn as much as possible to help me excel at
my job and/or interests, whether it be through reading trade magazines, attending seminars, perusing
related articles on the Internet, or talking with others
who have similar jobs and/or interests.

I know that faithfully doing these things will make
my way prosperous and help pave the way for soul
success.

_____
Signed

# Chapter Nine
# Tending to Your Spirit

A s we discussed in the last chapter, many people confuse the spirit and the soul. Since they are so intimately connected, some mistakenly believe that they are the same thing, neglecting to realize that spirit and soul are two separate entities. Here's a better way to understand the situation: The soul and spirit are sort of like Siamese twins. They are *separate* from each other, but closely *interconnected*. The Scriptures clarify this truth:

> *For the word of God is living and powerful, and sharper than any two-edged sword, piercing even to the division of soul and spirit, and of joints and marrow, and is a discerner of the thoughts and intents of the heart.* (Hebrews 4:12)

As this verse from Hebrews points out, the soul and spirit are separate, for God's word can pierce *"even to the division of soul and spirit."* The two can be divided. They are so closely connected, however, that separating them is like dividing joints from marrow.

*Pneuma,* the Greek word used for *spirit* in the New Testament, has many different meanings. It often refers to wind or breath, which are both invisible, just as the spirit of every man and woman is invisible. [1] Spirits do not have physical, flesh-like attributes. Rather, the spirit of man is the part that was created in God's image.

> *Then God said, "Let Us make man in Our image, according to Our likeness; let them have dominion over the fish of the sea, over the birds of the air, and over the cattle, over all the earth and over every creeping thing that creeps on the earth." So God created man in His own image; in the image of God He created him; male and female He created them.*
> (Genesis 1:26–27)

You must understand that when God said He made you in His image, He was not referring to physical attributes, such as hands, legs, feet, and arms. He was referring to the spiritual attributes and characteristics that He placed in you. For example, God is a ruler—in fact, He is the ultimate Ruler. *"The earth is the Lord's, and all its fullness, the world and those who dwell therein. For He has founded it upon the seas, and established it upon the waters"* (Psalm 24:1–2). When God created man in His image, He filled him with this attribute, the ability to rule: *"Let them have dominion over the fish of the sea, over the birds of the air, and over the cattle, over all the earth and over every creeping thing that creeps on the earth"* (Genesis 1:26). Similarly, God has fashioned man's spirit with the ability to create, to love, and to even feel sorrow, just as God creates, loves,

---

1. *Vine's Expository Dictionary of New Testament Words: A Comprehensive Dictionary of the Original Greek Words with Their Precise Meanings for English Readers,* Unabridged Edition (MacDonald Publishing Company), s.v. "spirit."

and feels sorrow. It is our spirits that have been made in His image.

The spirit of man is the truest, most real part of him, for it is the place where he has been created in the image of his Maker. Although the flesh at times seems to be more significant and far more real than the spirit, it's not. Naturally, most of us are "in touch" with our physical bodies, because our bodies are visible and tangible. When you need to blow your nose, you know it, and it doesn't take too long for you to figure out when you need a haircut either. Because you can see and feel your body, you're pretty in tune with its needs.

> The spirit of man is the truest, most real part of him—the image of his Maker.

But your physical makeup is not who you really are. You are not just the person you see in the mirror each morning, simply eyes, ears, mouth, and nose. The real you, the part that will last into eternity, can't be seen in the mirror. *"For the things which are seen are temporary, but the things which are not seen are eternal"* (2 Corinthians 4:18).

If we spend so much time attending to our physical bodies, which are temporal, by exercising, fixing our hair, and shopping for the perfect clothes, shouldn't we spend at least as much time on our spirits? The more we realize the importance of the spirit, the more we will be willing to invest into the development of our spirit-man.

## Spiritual Death

All of us are born spiritually dead. It's not that we're born without spirits but rather that our spirits are separated from the purpose for which they were initially created. God created us to have communion with Him, something that Adam and Eve enjoyed during their early days in Eden. However, once Adam and Eve disobeyed God by eating fruit from the

Tree of Knowledge of Good and Evil, the perfect fellowship they had once enjoyed with the Lord was completely severed.

> *And they heard the sound of the LORD God walking in the garden in the cool of the day, and Adam and his wife hid themselves from the presence of the LORD God among the trees of the garden. Then the LORD God called to Adam and said to him, "Where are you?" So he said, "I heard Your voice in the garden, and I was afraid because I was naked; and I hid myself." And He said, "Who told you that you were naked? Have you eaten from the tree of which I commanded you that you should not eat?"*
> (Genesis 3:8–11)

Notice what this passage tells us: After Adam and Eve sinned, they did not long for communion with the Lord as they had before. Instead, they immediately wanted to hide. There was now separation between God and man— between God's Spirit and man's spirit—a separation that was not there before. This event signified mankind's spiritual death, which God had forewarned Adam about:

> *And the LORD God commanded the man, saying, "Of every tree of the garden you may freely eat; but of the tree of the knowledge of good and evil you shall not eat, for in the day that you eat of it you shall surely die."*
> (Genesis 2:16–17)

God clearly told Adam that if he ate the fruit, he would die that very same day. Many are thus confused when they learn that Adam lived to be 930 years old: *"So all the days that Adam lived were nine hundred and thirty years; and he died"* (Genesis 5:5). How, they ask, did he live to be 930 if he was supposed to die the same day? The answer is that

Adam spiritually died that day. Along with this spiritual death came eventual physical death, but physical death was nothing compared to spiritual death since spiritual death meant complete and total separation from God.

## Spiritual Rebirth

Fortunately, God didn't abandon man as spiritually dead forever. Instead, He sent His Son, Jesus Christ, as a mediator between God and man. When Jesus came to earth, died on the cross, and rose again on the third day, He reopened the doorway for pure and perfect communion with God. Christ conquered the sin that had controlled our lives, and He broke, once and for all, the control that death had had on our spirits. No longer would there be a huge barrier between God and man. Because of Christ's death and resurrection, the deplorable sin that once controlled our spirits and separated us from a perfect, holy God, was banished. With Christ came the opportunity to be spiritually alive once more.

How do we accept this new spiritual life? In other words, how can we be restored to right fellowship with our God? A prison guard asked Paul and Silas this same question in the New Testament:

*But at midnight Paul and Silas were praying and singing hymns to God, and the prisoners were listening to them. Suddenly there was a great earthquake, so that the foundations of the prison were shaken; and immediately all the doors were opened and everyone's chains were loosed. And the keeper of the prison, awaking from sleep and seeing the prison doors open, supposing the prisoners had fled, drew his sword and was about to kill himself. But Paul called with a loud voice, saying, "Do yourself no harm, for we are all here." Then he called for a light, ran in, and fell down trembling before Paul and Silas. And he brought them out and said, "Sirs, what must I do to be saved?" So they said, "Believe on the Lord Jesus Christ, and you will be saved, you and your household."* (Acts 16:25–31)

We see from this passage that belief is key. Once we recognize our complete separation from God and understand Jesus' role as bridging this separation, we must believe. As Paul taught in Romans, we are also called to confess our belief to others.

*If you confess with your mouth the Lord Jesus and believe in your heart that God has raised Him from the dead, you will be saved. For with the heart one believes unto righteousness, and with the mouth confession is made unto salvation.* (Romans 10:9–10)

Have you accepted Jesus Christ as your Savior? Have you believed on Him to spiritually renew and revive you, and have you confessed this belief to others? Until you have done this, you are spiritually dead. If you have not yet accepted Christ as your Savior, will you do so now? Simply tell Him that you realize your sinfulness and recognize that you are spiritually dead and separated from Him. Let Him know that you do not desire to remain spiritually dead, but rather desire the life that only He can give you through spiritual rebirth. Ask Him now to forgive your sins, and believe that He has done so. When you do this, you become spiritually alive, just as Adam and Eve were before they sinned! You can begin enjoying perfect communion with God and have the assurance that you will be with Him in heaven for eternity.

A popular movie came out in the mid-'90s called *Dead Man Walking*. Maybe you've seen it. It's about a nun who befriends a convicted murderer on Death Row and the emotional struggles she faces as she wrestles with the ethics of capital punishment. I like the movie, but I like the title even more, because "dead man walking" perfectly describes the person who has yet to accept Christ's spiritual renewal. Are you a dead man or woman walking? Do you go through every day thinking you're alive while all along the truest part of you, your spirit, is dead?

## Once You're Reborn...

If you have already accepted Christ's gift of new life and are no longer a "dead man walking," do you continue to seek after the growth of your spirit-man? Do you invest in the health of your spirit, just as you invest in the health of your soul and body? Or do you leave it to chance, hoping that, somehow, your relationship with God will continue to grow no matter how much or how little effort you put into it?

The Bible tells the story of a man named Job, and this story helps us understand the importance of protecting and strengthening our spirit-man. Job, the Scripture says, walked blamelessly before God. *"There was a man in the land of Uz, whose name was Job; and that man was blameless and upright, and one who feared God and shunned evil"* (Job 1:1). Job was a man of God who sought after the Lord and humbly repented whenever He did wrong in the Lord's sight. Clearly Job was not sinless, for the only person who never sinned was Jesus Christ. *"All have sinned and fall short of the glory of God"* (Romans 3:23). When the Scripture says Job *"was blameless and upright,"* it means that Job's life was characterized by obedience, which greatly pleased the Lord.

> The person who has yet to accept Christ's spiritual renewal is truly a "dead man walking."

Satan saw Job's faithfulness as a challenge and immediately told God that the only reason Job was so faithful was because God had placed a hedge of protection around him.

"If You remove the hedge," Satan said, in essence, "Job will curse You. You just wait and see." The devil thought Job was in his relationship with God solely for the money and the material prosperity he could receive: *"You have blessed the work of his hands, and his possessions have increased in the land. But now, stretch out Your hand and touch all that he has, and he will surely curse You to Your face!"* (Job 1:10–11).

God knew His servant Job better than Satan did, though, and He knew that Satan had misrepresented Job's character. So He allowed Satan to trouble Job's life by interfering with Job's businesses, assets, and family. God wouldn't let Satan harm Job's health, however. *"Behold, all that he has is in your power; only do not lay a hand on his person"* (Job 1:12).

Satan gleefully set out on his mission to ruin Job's life, certain that Job would eventually betray God. Soon, one tragedy after another was reported to Job. First, he lost his servants, then his livestock, and next his herdsman. Finally, all his children were killed. Although Job did not understand why misfortune was coming upon him, he continued to love God and to seek Him for comfort and relief. Contrary to Satan's prediction for Job, God's servant remained completely faithful to his Lord:

> *And he said: "Naked I came from my mother's womb, and naked shall I return there. The LORD gave, and the LORD has taken away; blessed be the name of the LORD." In all this Job did not sin nor charge God with wrong.* (Job 1:21–22)

## Access to the Spirit

Bewildered by Job's commitment to God, Satan dug around trying to find some other excuse for why Job stayed true to his Maker. Finally, he came up with something.

"You've not only prospered Job with material riches and a wonderful family," Satan essentially said, "but you've also graced him with great physical health and strength." The devil then asked God for permission to afflict Job's body, sure that Job would then turn against his Lord. God granted permission, under one condition. *"And the LORD said to Satan, 'Behold, he is in your hand, but spare his life'"* (Job 2:6).

Many people interpret this commandment as God telling Satan not to kill Job, or take his *physical* life. This is the most readily apparent meaning, and probably the most widely accepted. But I think the word *"life"* has another meaning here, as well. I am convinced that God was also forbidding Satan to touch Job's *spirit* life. In other words, God was concerned that Satan not have access to Job's spirit. God was essentially saying, "Do whatever you want to Job, to his possessions, to his family, even to his body. But do not touch his  life, especially his spirit life, for his life is Mine."

If you're like me, you turn on your radio almost every day. I turn it on in the car, at work, and sometimes at home. Through the radio, I can listen to music, talk shows, and news updates as they are broadcast from a radio tower directly to my radio's antenna. These radio transmissions are always being broadcast, but if I do not have my radio turned on and tuned in to the right station, I won't be able to receive them.

The spirit-man works much the same way. It is through the spirit that God communicates with us. It is His avenue for speaking to man, for it is the innermost part of man. *"The spirit of a man is the lamp of the LORD, searching all the inner depths of his heart"* (Proverbs 20:27). Since our spirits are the means by which God speaks to us, He desires for our spirits to be completely reserved for Him.

Since Job belonged to God, God had claim to Job's spirit, just as God has claim to the spirits of all His children. Satan had no right to interfere with Job's spirit, for this was God's realm. Since Job was a child of God, God alone had the right to "broadcast" to his spirit.

The same is true for us. If you are a son or daughter of God, your spirit belongs to Him. As Proverbs 20:27 says, it is through your spirit that the Lord searches and speaks to your heart. Your spirit is His possession, and nothing can interfere with that.

> *Who shall separate us from the love of Christ? Shall tribulation, or distress, or persecution, or famine, or nakedness, or peril, or sword? As it is written: "For Your sake we are killed all day long; we are accounted as sheep for the slaughter." Yet in all these things we are more than conquerors through Him who loved us. For I am persuaded that neither death nor life, nor angels nor principalities nor powers, nor things present nor things to come, nor height nor depth, nor any other created thing, shall be able to separate us from the love of God which is in Christ Jesus our Lord.*
> (Romans 8:35–39)

You can, however, make decisions that compromise the clarity of communication between God's Spirit and your spirit. Just as putting down the antenna of a radio compromises the clarity of the communications the radio receives, certain behaviors in the Christian's life can cause his spirit to be less "in tune" with the Lord.

Are you keeping your spiritual antenna up? Are you taking time to pray, read God's Word, and meditate on things of the Lord? Or have you lowered your antenna, choosing instead to leave your spiritual growth to chance?

# Making a Meaningful Commitment

Since your spirit is so important, make a commitment now to feed and protect it.

As with my soul, I will feed my spirit with God's Word. His Word gives me life, purpose, and meaning as it instructs me how to serve Him more fully and bring glory to His name. For these reasons, I will receive daily portions of His Word into my spirit, and, in keeping with Psalm 119:11, commit His Word to memory: *"Your word I have hidden in my heart, That I might not sin against You!"*

Since my spirit is my communication lifeline with the Lord, I will make sure that I have daily conversations with Him through prayer. Realizing that communication is always a two-way street, I will not only regularly talk to God but will also listen to Him, knowing that He responds to me when I call.

Since my flesh continually wars against my spirit, I will daily choose to die to my flesh, so that the Spirit of God can have His way with me. Like Paul, who wrote, *"I affirm, by the boasting in you which I have in Christ Jesus our Lord, I die daily"* (1 Corinthians 15:31), I will crucify my flesh each day so that my spirit may be more in tune with the Lord and His desires for my spirit-man.

---

Signed

# Part III

---

# Maintaining Your Solid Foundation: Forgive and Forget

# Introduction

I f you've ever owned a house, you probably know that certain things destroy a foundation and must be avoided. Water, for instance, can cause major structural damage, as can termites, mildew, and extreme temperatures. If a homeowner wants his foundation to last any length of time, he should take action to avoid such "destroyers." He might put drains in around the house to avoid flooding and excess moisture, treat the house for termites, and insulate the walls to protect them from temperature changes.

The foundations of our lives are no different. Certain things can seep in and threaten to undo our carefully constructed groundwork. Perhaps the biggest of these is Unforgiveness—and his close relative, Unforgetting. I'm sure you've seen them both, either in your own life or in the lives of those close to you. Unforgiveness is that spirit that simply refuses to forgive, choosing instead to constantly remember and replay those things that should be forgotten. Perhaps you've been there. Your spouse says words that wound you so deeply that you secretly vow never to forget them—and never to let your spouse forget them, either. Or, your best friend betrays you, and you make a point of paying her back by betraying her at every opportunity you're given. Or, in perhaps the most common and widespread unforgiveness of all, you refuse to forgive yourself. Maybe you sinned in some way, or you let someone down in your life, and although you've been assured of God's forgiveness, you simply cannot forgive yourself.

Jesus taught a lot about unforgiveness. In His Sermon on the Mount, He taught about the negative effects of unforgiveness on prayer: *"For if you forgive men their trespasses, your heavenly Father will also forgive you. But if you do not forgive men their trespasses, neither will your Father forgive your trespasses"* (Matthew 6:14–15). *"Therefore be merciful, just as your Father also is merciful. Judge not, and you shall not be judged. Condemn not, and you shall not be condemned. Forgive, and you will be forgiven"* (Luke 6:36–37). At another point, He reminded us of the importance of forgiveness by instructing us to *repeatedly* forgive those who hurt us: *"Then Peter came to Him and said, 'Lord, how often shall my brother sin against me, and I forgive him? Up to seven times?' Jesus said to him, 'I do not say to you, up to seven times, but up to seventy times seven'"* (Matthew 18:21–22).

Forgiving and forgetting are by no means "normal" by this world's standards. The natural reaction when we've been hurt is to feel mad and stay mad. Forgiveness simply does not come easily. For a Christian, however, unforgiveness is abnormal behavior, and forgiving should be "the norm." To not forgive is to directly disobey the Lord and His commandments.

When we choose to not forgive, the bitter fruit of unforgiveness manifests itself in multiple ways in our lives. Like cancer, it spreads, quickly infecting other areas of our lives with bitterness, anger, and resentment. As we choose to ignore it and refuse to take care of it, its grip on our lives intensifies. With each passing treatment-less day, unforgiveness gains more ground and begins to affect those around us, too, as they must cope with the sad effects of cancerous unforgiveness on our lives.

The fortunate thing is that, like cancer, an unforgiving spirit can be detected and dealt with before it becomes full-blown. This can save your life—and the lives of those around you.

Refusing to forgive a brother, a sister, or even one's self, however, can lead to a lifetime of grief and spiritual decline. Similarly, refusing to forget failures can start the process of gradual foundational decay. Unforgiveness and unforgetting—like termites, basement floods, and huge foundational cracks—can threaten to destroy our lives' solid foundations. We do well to take preventative measures against unforgiveness and unforgetting. To not do so is to doom our carefully laid foundations to crumbling, erosion, and eventual destruction.

# Chapter Ten
# Forgetting Yourself

I n my many years as a pastor, I have dealt with thousands of people who have come to me with confessions of sins committed in years past. Sometimes the sin has been adultery, abortion, stealing, or lying. No matter what the sin was, however, these people sought help because they could not forgive themselves. Although they had asked God to forgive them, and although they believed that He had forgiven them, they still faced constant internal battles. On a daily basis, they beat themselves up, refusing to forget the sin that God had already laid to rest: *"As far as the east is from the west, so far has He removed our transgressions from us"* (Psalm 103:12). No matter how hard they tried, they simply could not forgive themselves.

How tragic it is when we choose not to forgive ourselves! We are our own worst critics, oftentimes harder on ourselves than anyone else is on us. Satan uses this to keep us down—to stop us from building lasting, structurally sound, stable foundations. If we allow it, his diabolical plans can sabotage our relationships and endeavors as our foundations crumble underneath the weight of unforgiveness. When we do choose to forgive, however, strong, sturdy, and lasting foundations are the end result.

## Might You Need to Move?

Before accepting Christ on the Damascus road, Paul (then named Saul) was notorious for persecuting Christian believers. He thought Christianity to be a corrupt and cultic faith, believing Jesus to be a fraud and imposter who came to invalidate the Jewish religion. He persecuted many people for their faith in Christ, sincerely believing that such behavior was righteous and God-ordained. Fueled by mad ignorance, he went forth, persecuting in the name of God and even approving as others actually killed Christians.

One day, however, the Lord confronted Saul in a blinding light and a voice from heaven. In this sacred moment, Saul realized the truth and repented—meaning his thoughts and actions took a 180-degree turn. No longer did he see his persecutory acts as righteous, or even acceptable. From that moment onward, his thoughts and actions were completely renewed, and he got a new name to go along with it. Paul's own telling of his conversion is found in Acts:

> *Now it happened, as I journeyed and came near Damascus at about noon, suddenly a great light from heaven shone around me. And I fell to the ground and heard a voice saying to me, "Saul, Saul, why are you persecuting Me?" So I answered, "Who are You, Lord?" And He said to me, "I am Jesus of Nazareth, whom you are persecuting." And those who were with me indeed saw the light and were afraid, but they did not hear the voice of Him who spoke to me. So I said, "What shall I do, Lord?" And the Lord said*

*to me, "Arise and go into Damascus, and there you will be told all things which are appointed for you to do."* (Acts 22:6–10)

Paul then proceeded to Damascus where he met a Christian named Ananias, who prayed for Paul, helped restore Paul's sight, and then informed Paul of his next assignment:

*Then a certain Ananias, a devout man according to the law, having a good testimony with all the Jews who dwelt there, came to me; and he stood and said to me, "Brother Saul, receive your sight." And at that same hour I looked up at him. Then he said, "The God of our fathers has chosen you that you should know His will, and see the Just One, and hear the voice of His mouth. For you will be His witness to all men of what you have seen and heard. And now why are you waiting? Arise and be baptized, and wash away your sins, calling on the name of the Lord."* (Acts 22:12–16)

Clearly the Lord forgave Paul's sins and chose to forget his past failures. The Lord realized, however, that man was not as quick to forgive and forget as He was. *"As far as the east is from the west"* is a pretty far distance—often too far for mankind to handle. God knew that Paul's peers would have a tough time forgiving and forgetting all the grief Paul had caused by persecuting so many Christians, so He commanded Paul to go elsewhere: *"Now it happened, when I returned to Jerusalem and was praying in the temple, that I was in a trance and saw Him saying to me, 'Make haste and get out of Jerusalem quickly, for they will not receive your testimony concerning Me'"* (Acts 22:17–18).

At first, Paul had his doubts. Could he ever escape his infamy?

*So I said, "Lord, they know that in every synagogue I imprisoned and beat those who believe on You. And when the blood of Your martyr Stephen was shed, I also was standing by consenting to his death, and guarding the clothes of those who were killing him."*

(Acts 22:19–20)

God, however, was patient with Paul, and promised to protect him if Paul would only obey: *"Depart,"* the Lord said to Paul, *"for I will send you far from here to the Gentiles"* (Acts 22:21).

While God's commandment for Paul to leave Jerusalem was in part for Paul's own safety, I believe it was also for the preservation of his peace of mind. Jerusalem held great religious and moral significance for Paul, as it did for all Jews, and it was undoubtedly difficult for Paul to leave. Had he stayed in Jerusalem, however, grief, heartache, and guilt might have plagued him daily as he passed the places where he once persecuted Christians and as he saw the anguished faces of those whose loved ones he had witnessed being killed. God realized that if Paul stayed in Jerusalem, his ministry would be over before it even began. How could Paul move forward in life if he was constantly bombarded by painful reminders of his past?

I venture to say that many of you reading this are in similar situations of your own. Maybe you didn't persecute others like Paul did, but you did bring pain to those around you— pain for which you have a hard time forgiving yourself now. Your surroundings and the people you see serve as continual reminders of what a wicked, unforgiveable person you feel you are. In such a situation, you have a hard time accepting the Lord's gracious forgiveness, much less forgiving yourself as well. Far too many people remain terribly dysfunctional, distraught, and disabled because of situations like this.

For Paul, the solution was to leave Jerusalem. For you, it may mean leaving New York, Los Angeles, Detroit, Memphis, India, China, Russia, or Ghana. Maybe it means cutting off certain relationships that prevent you from forgiving yourself and thus moving on in service to the Lord. Or maybe it simply means daily reminding yourself that God has forgiven you and that you should, too!

Whatever the situation, do not allow yourself to swim in a sea of unforgiveness or wallow in pain from the past. Instead, move on, doing whatever it takes to do so.

## The Fruits of Failure

Please be assured that past failures and faults do not have to be fatal. In fact, failure has actually served as a catapult in the lives of many people, launching them to accomplishment and success. Consider Thomas Alva Edison, for instance. Edison invented the phonograph, the motion picture camera, and—his best-known invention—the incandescent lightbulb. In fact, Edison held more than one thousand different patents, and many of these inventions continue to impact the everyday lives of people in our world today. Not everything Thomas Edison invented was a success, though. In fact, some of his inventions failed miserably.

One concept that never took off was Edison's interest in multiple uses for concrete. In 1899 he formed the Edison Portland Cement Co. and started making everything from cabinets to pianos to houses out of concrete. At the time, however, cement was far too costly for the average person, and most of Edison's concrete concepts flopped as a result.

But Edison didn't give up on cement, despite the sense of failure he undoubtedly felt. Eventually his company was hired to build Yankee Stadium in the Bronx, and think of how many things are made of cement today! Edison did not dwell on his failure, but rather used it as motivation toward greater success. In this way, he always kept moving forward.

## Don't Get Stuck on Success

Just as we can be consumed by our failures, we can be distracted by successes, too. The greatest hindrance to your success may very well be past successes. I've seen many people get stuck on past successes to the point where they lose interest in pursuing future successes. So what if you were the star of your high school basketball team; what are you the star of now? Who cares if you have the greatest standing track record at your old college; what records have you tried breaking recently? Praise God that He worked through you to save seven people five years ago, but are you so consumed by this that you've neglected to keep telling the Good News of Christ to those around you? Sometimes past successes can hinder where God is trying to take you now.

> Sometimes past successes can hinder where God is trying to take you now.

One reason I believe God has used me to build such a great ministry is that as soon as I have completed one project, I move on to the next one. I am grateful that God has taught me this principle of "pressing on," for it has yielded great fruit in our church. After our 3,400-seat cathedral was built, for instance, I joined my congregation in experiencing their joy and excitement, but I also turned to God and asked Him, "What's next?" My mind was already turning toward our family life center that would house full-court basketball, a complete workout and fitness facility, an Olympic-sized swimming pool, and a racquetball court. My thoughts were already geared toward building some kind of first-class senior citizens' housing. My attention was already directed toward additional parking and the possibility of expanding our present sanctuary so that more people could come and hear God's Word. I refused—and continue to refuse—to get hung up on past successes.

# The Blessing of "Amnesia"

If we are to maintain solid foundations in the Lord, sometimes we will have to forget the past, along with its failures and accomplishments, its faults and perfections. Having an "amnesia," of sorts, can be a tremendous blessing, for it allows us to move forward no matter what's in the past. Paul experienced such "amnesia" in his own life. To the believers at Philippi, he wrote,

> *Brethren, I do not count myself to have apprehended; but one thing I do, forgetting those things which are behind and reaching forward to those things which are ahead, I press toward the goal for the prize of the upward call of God in Christ Jesus.*
> (Philippians 3:13–14)

Maybe you've never thought of memory loss as a blessing. Our society is so concerned these days with improving our memories that there are all kinds of memory-enhancing nutritional supplements available, as well as special mind exercises to keep our memories sharp and in shape. But when it comes to certain things—to those things that consume our thoughts and energy so much that we are immobilized—memory loss is a blessing.

Think about Paul. Not only did he have a painful past that he did well to leave behind; he also had a past of accomplishments that very easily could have become a source of pride and distraction for him. He was an educated man, a scholar of scholars. If anyone had cause to dwell on the past, it was Paul. His second letter to the Corinthians emphasized this when Paul pretended to boast in his past accomplishments:

*I say again, let no one think me a fool. If otherwise, at least receive me as a fool, that I also may boast a little. What I speak, I speak not according to the Lord, but as it were, foolishly, in this confidence of boasting. Seeing that many boast according to the flesh, I also will boast....But in whatever anyone is bold; I speak foolishly; I am bold also. Are they Hebrews? So am I. Are they Israelites? So am I. Are they the seed of Abraham? So am I. Are they ministers of Christ?; I speak as a fool; I am more.*
(2 Corinthians 11:16–18; 21–23)

Paul wasn't really boasting. Notice how he said, *"I speak as a fool."* He realized the foolishness of dwelling on the past—both its good and its bad points—and he refused to do so. If anyone had cause to dwell on the past and pridefully revel in all God had accomplished through him, it was Paul. But he chose not to. Instead, he chose to push onward: *"Brethren, I do not count myself to have apprehended; but one thing I do, forgetting those things which are behind and reaching forward to those things which are ahead, I press toward the goal for the prize of the upward call of God in Christ Jesus"* (Philippians 3:13–14).

> The blessing of "amnesia" is being able to forget what is behind so we can press on toward the goal.

This is the blessing of "amnesia," being able to forget all that's behind so we can press forward toward the goal God has set for us instead. This great secret was the *"one thing"* Paul claimed to know with confidence about successfully living the Christian life, and it was this *"one thing"* he so earnestly wanted to pass on to others.

Think about all that Paul was able to accomplish in his lifetime. The Holy Spirit penned nearly two-thirds of our New Testament writings through him. He established and oversaw churches within many Gentile communities throughout Europe and Asia. He preached the name of the Lord to many great metropolitan cities and saw many saved as a result. But Paul would not have been able to do any of these things if he had not already done one thing—forget. By forgetting those things that were behind him—failures and accomplishments—he was able to reach forward to the things that were before him.

Imagine putting your car into reverse, backing up, suddenly pulling your transmission lever into drive, and then accelerating without first giving your transmission a chance to change gears. What would happen? You'd probably destroy the transmission!

Or suppose you tried walking forward while your head was turned around, looking backward. Would you get too far? Probably not. Most likely you would run into something first, or something else would run into you. You need to focus on the goal before you if you are to arrive at that goal. Not only that, you need to make sure that all your gears are pushing *forward* toward that goal.

Forget the stuff behind you, good and bad alike. You can *think* on these things and learn from them, but don't *dwell* on them. Dwelling gets you stuck in the past and ultimately starts chipping away at your foundation. When it comes to your own failures and successes, forgive and forget, for this will go a long way toward maintaining the solid foundation of your life.

# Chapter Eleven
# Forgiving Others

We have all heard people say, "Oh, I'll forgive so-and-so, but I'll never forget what they did to me." Such forgiveness is really not forgiveness at all, for true forgiveness always has an element of forgetting. Henry Ward Beecher, a nineteenth-century clergyman, abolitionist, and orator, said this about forgiveness: "'I can forgive, but I cannot forget,' is only another way of saying, 'I will not forgive.' Forgiveness ought to be like a cancelled note—torn in two, and burned up, so that it never can be shown against one." [1]

You see, true forgiveness means clearing the slate. It means letting the person who wronged you start over again—without you constantly reminding them of the times they hurt you. You cannot genuinely forgive a person and yet keep records of their offenses.

Perhaps you've seen marriages, friendships, or family relationships where a person claims to have forgiven another but that individual's actions continue to scream, "I

1. Notable Quotables. <http://www.geocities.com/notablequotables1/BEECHER.html> (9 April, 2003)

don't forgive you at all!" Such people forgive only in words and then continue to punish the person who pained them by continually bringing up the painful past. I think you'd agree with me that such relationships are not healthy and ultimately end up harming both people involved. Relationships like this do not build up the people involved but constantly tear both of them down instead.

As with all things in the Christian life, the best place to go if we want to learn about forgiveness is Jesus Christ Himself. His example of forgiveness, along with the parables He told about forgiveness, should serve as our foundation as we seek to forgive others to the fullest.

## A Horrible Hypothetical...and a Fantastic Fact

What if God remembered your past sins? What if, every morning, He reminded you of *every sin* you'd ever committed, even though He said He had already forgiven you? Would you feel forgiven? Of course not! The same principle holds true concerning our relationships with people, too. When we're reminded of our failures, we feel everything *but* forgiven. Forgetting goes hand-in-hand with forgiving.

> When we're reminded of our failures, we feel everything but forgiven. We must also learn to forget.

Praise God that He doesn't drudge up our sins every day. When we're forgiven, we're forgiven. Period. *"As far as the east is from the west, so far has He removed our transgressions from us"* (Psalm 103:12). He completely separates our sins from us and remembers them no more!

Is this possible? Does God really have a sort of "amnesia" Himself? Please understand that God *could* remember your sins if He chose to—but the amazing thing is, He chooses not to! Jesus' blood sacrifice completely blotted out your sins, and God has vowed to remember the sins of His children no more.

> *"For this is the covenant that I will make with the house of Israel after those days," says the LORD: "I will put My laws in their mind and write them on their hearts; and I will be their God, and they shall be My people. None of them shall teach his neighbor, and none his brother, saying, 'Know the LORD,' for all shall know Me, from the least of them to the greatest of them. For I will be merciful to their unrighteousness, and their sins and their lawless deeds I will remember no more." In that He says, "A new covenant," He has made the first obsolete. Now what is becoming obsolete and growing old is ready to vanish away.* (Hebrews 8:10–13)

In this new covenant—of which we, as Christians, are a part—the Lord *"remember[s] no more"* our sins and transgressions. As His children, we are called to extend this same degree of forgiveness to those who hurt us.

## The Forgiveness Factor

Jesus made it very clear to His disciples that forgiving others was an important and inevitable part of the Christian life. Consider this conversation that He had with Peter: *"Then Peter came to Him and said, 'Lord, how often shall my brother sin against me, and I forgive him? Up to seven times?' Jesus said to him, 'I do not say to you, up to seven times, but up to seventy times seven'"* (Matthew 18:21–22). What did Jesus mean by this? Did He mean, literally, that Peter was supposed to say, "I forgive you," seventy times seven (or 490) times, whenever somebody sinned against him? Probably not. Instead, the Lord was simply emphasizing the Christian's responsibility to forgive his brother, no matter what. In other words, if your brother sins against you 490 times, then you forgive him 490 times! Or, if your brother sins only once against you but continues to ask you 490 times, "Do you forgive me?" then it is your job to assure him of your forgiveness every one of those 490 times that he asks!

I learned this lesson firsthand during my early years of ministry. I eventually dubbed the principle that I gleaned from these learning experiences "the forgiveness factor." I define it as such: *The forgiveness factor is allowing for the fact that, in any relationship, we will be required to forgive, perhaps even many times.*

If you cannot accept this truth, then you're not ready to enter into a marriage, a close friendship, or even a business partnership. Being hurt by others is an inevitable part of life, and forgiving is really the only way to move on. If you're not ready to forgive, you're only setting yourself up for failure.

As I said before, I learned the forgiveness factor in a very real way during my first years of marriage—not because I had to repeatedly forgive my wife, but because she had to repeatedly forgive me. Aside from Jesus Christ, Mrs. Reathie Bailey has taught me more about forgiveness than anyone else.

For more than twenty-seven years, I have had the pleasure—and I do mean pleasure—of being married to this incredibly patient and forgiving woman of God. In the early years of our marriage, I had a lot to learn all at once—how to lead a congregation, how to be a good husband, and how to be a caring father. I was pretty clueless when it came to a lot of things, and I ended up making some very bad decisions and foolish choices. (I still don't know it all, but by the grace of God, I'm learning more each day.)

Through all of this, Reathie did not judge or condemn me, but simply forgave me from the start. I can remember her saying, "I don't want to talk about it at all. I forgive you." She didn't want to discuss the details of my bad decisions to make me feel guiltier than I already did. Instead, she forgave me, and laid each situation to rest.

Some people might think that such an approach would leave me feeling shameless, unconvicted, and consequently not cautious enough about making more bad decisions in the future. The truth, though, is that exactly the opposite was true. Reathie's unconditional love compelled me to love her even more by making decisions that would benefit our congregation, our family, and our marriage. In my mind, it

> Being hurt is an inevitable part of life, and forgiving is the only way to move on.

became unacceptable to do anything that would displease the one who had so willingly forgiven me. Reathie's loving forgiveness served as a sort of accountability, encouraging me to pursue extra wisdom, care, and thoughtfulness whenever it came to making decisions.

## The Ultimate Forgiveness

Maybe you have someone in your life like my Reathie, someone who has forgiven you, time and time again, even when you felt like you didn't deserve it. Such people can serve as wonderful examples as we learn how to extend forgiveness to others. The supreme example, however, is found in only one person—Jesus Christ.

Forgiveness was no small deal for God. You see, sin is so offensive and deplorable to God that He cannot bear to look at it. *"You are of purer eyes than to behold evil, and cannot look on wickedness"* (Habakkuk 1:13). Forgiving us cost God dearly—the price of His only Son's life, in fact. This is the ultimate example of forgiveness.

When we realize the price He has paid for our forgiveness, our whole perspective should change. I cannot help but think of God with greater awe, amazement, reverence, and respect whenever I consider His forgiveness of my sins. What a huge debt He had to pay!

Jesus talked about this in one of His parables, the parable of the ungrateful servant. It starts like this:

> *Therefore the kingdom of heaven is like a certain king who wanted to settle accounts with his servants. And when he had begun to settle accounts, one was brought to him who owed him ten thousand talents. But as he was not able to pay, his master commanded that he be sold, with his wife and children and all that he had, and that payment be made. The servant therefore fell down before him, saying, "Master, have patience with me, and I will pay you all." Then the master of that servant was moved with compassion, released him, and forgave him the debt.* (Matthew 18:23–27)

This part of the parable describes our relationship with God. Just as the servant owed the king a huge debt, so too are we greatly indebted to God, our King. The amount spoken of here, *"ten thousand talents,"* is a large chunk of cash. Translated into our time and currency, it would probably add up to be several million dollars. Paying off such a debt would be impossible for any servant! The same is true in our lives. The debt we owe God because of our sins is something that we cannot pay off. Just like the servant in this parable, our debt can only be pardoned by mercy from our King.

Now, you'd think that this servant would be so grateful because the king pardoned his debt that he would respond by extending mercy to others. Unfortunately, this wasn't the case.

> *But that servant went out and found one of his fellow servants who owed him a hundred denarii; and he laid hands on him and took him by the throat, saying, "Pay me what you owe!" So his fellow servant fell down at his feet and begged him, saying, "Have patience with me, and I will pay you all." And he would not, but went and threw him into prison till he should pay the debt.*
> (Matthew 18:28–30)

Instead of pardoning a fellow servant's debt, the unmerciful servant in this parable chose to be unforgiving and relentless. What's even more pitiful is that this debt was so small compared to the one the king had forgiven. *"One hundred denarii"* translates into just a few dollars in our time. Can you imagine? This servant had just been pardoned for millions of dollars and yet could not find mercy enough to pardon a fellow servant's debt of only a few bucks. This hardly seems right.

> The Lord has pardoned your gigantic debt in the greatest display of forgiveness ever.

Sadly, this is what many of us do every day when we choose to perpetuate a spirit of unforgiveness. If you are a Christian, the Lord has cleared your life of a gigantic debt. He has pardoned you in the greatest display of forgiveness ever. If this is true, then why do we so often refuse to forgive the small debts others owe to us? When we consider the supreme forgiveness that God has shown us, our response should be one of gratefulness to God and overflowing forgiveness for others.

Do you remember the principle of sowing and reaping that we discussed earlier in this book? Well, this same principle extends into the realm of forgiveness. If I sow forgiveness, then I will reap forgiveness from others. If I fail to forgive, however, then I will have to face unforgiving spirits from others. The end of Jesus' parable brings this point home.

*So when his fellow servants saw what had been done, they were very grieved, and came and told their master all that had been done. Then his master, after he had called him, said to him, "You wicked servant! I forgave you all that debt because you begged me. Should you not also have had compassion on your fellow servant, just as I had pity on you?" And his master was angry, and delivered him to the torturers until he should pay all that was due to him. So My heavenly Father also will do to you if each of you, from his heart, does not forgive his brother his trespasses.*
(Matthew 18:31–35)

If you want to taste forgiveness in your life, you must be willing to be a forgiver first. Remember, no debt is too great to pardon, for God has already paid off the greatest debt of all—our sins. In light of His abundant forgiveness, surely we can forgive others.

# Chapter Twelve

# Forgiveness Now

We live in a very feelings-oriented society. We are continually bombarded with the message that we should pursue whatever "feels good" at the moment, no matter what the consequences might be later on. Don't feel like going to work today? Then stay home! Feel like buying that new $200 coat that you've been drooling over, even though you don't need one and you really can't afford it? Go ahead! Buy it anyway if you feel like it! Or do you feel like going out for drinks with that coworker who's been flirting with you lately, even though you know it might lead to unfaithfulness to your spouse? Don't worry about it! If you feel like going out for drinks, then by all means, go out!

Unfortunately, this mentality runs deep in our society, and it has seeped into many realms of everyday life. Even when it comes to forgiveness, we often avoid it simply because we don't "feel" forgiving. Have you found yourself in this situation? Even though someone has apologized to you, you're still angry with that person and just can't seem find it in your heart to forgive him or her.

However, the fact of the matter is that we may never completely *feel* like forgiving. We may always hurt because of what was done to us, and perhaps our hearts will never feel a rush of forgiveness toward the person who has wronged us. When this happens, are we to respond by simply not forgiving? No. Instead, we must *choose* to forgive.

There's a famous song by the Christian band dc talk called "Luv Is a Verb." The song talks about how love is not just a feeling, but rather something that we show to others through our actions and behavior. Love is something that we must choose to do, even when we feel far from loving toward someone. The same thing can be said for forgiveness. Forgiving is a verb. It's something we must *do*. It is not a feeling, an emotion, or a sentiment that comes into our hearts every now and then when we're lucky. Instead, it is a choice that we make, a choice that shows through our actions, attitudes, and behaviors toward that person who has hurt us.

> Forgiveness is not a feeling or an emotion. It is a choice we make.

I don't recall ever seeing a Scripture verse that said, "Forgive others when you feel like it," or "Forgive only if you feel forgiving." On the contrary, almost all the Scripture passages dealing with forgiveness are commandments to forgive, no matter how we are feeling.

*And whenever you stand praying, if you have anything against anyone, forgive him, that your Father in heaven may also forgive you your trespasses. But if you do not forgive, neither will your Father in heaven forgive your trespasses.* (Mark 11:25–26)

*Judge not, and you shall not be judged. Condemn not, and you shall not be condemned. Forgive, and you will be forgiven.* (Luke 6:37)

*Take heed to yourselves. If your brother sins against you, rebuke him; and if he repents, forgive him. And if he sins against you seven times in a day, and seven times in a day returns to you, saying, "I repent," you shall forgive him.* (Luke 17:3–4)

Please, don't misunderstand me. I'm not saying that forgiveness shouldn't be heartfelt. In fact, Matthew 18:35 tells us that when we forgive our brothers and sisters in Christ, we are to forgive "from the heart." Our forgiveness must always be sincere. However, oftentimes we will still feel anger and resentment. Does this mean we should hold out on forgiving until these feelings relent? No. We must still forgive, as soon as possible. We can then confess our lingering hurt to God and ask that He purify it from our hearts. Often, simply choosing to treat the person in love and forgiveness brings our hearts closer to actually feeling that forgiveness.

## Before the Sun Goes Down

Why does God care so much about how long it takes us to forgive? Big deal if we wait it out till next week when we don't feel quite so angry, right? Well, the truth is, it is a big deal. Ephesians 4:26–27 says, *"Be angry, and do not sin': do not let the sun go down on your wrath, nor give place to the devil"* (Ephesians 4:26–27). God knows how the human heart works. When we try to "wait it out," we inevitably end up even angrier. It's very easy to end up sinning in our anger. If we don't settle matters right away, we give the devil a foothold in our lives.

This reminds us just how powerful unforgiveness is. When we don't let go of our resentment right away, then unforgiveness festers in our hearts, eventually manifesting itself in acts of bitterness and sinful anger. Additionally, the longer we wait to be reconciled to the person who has hurt us, the more we harm our relationship with that person. It is crucial that we forgive right away.

## Hatefulness Brings Hurt, Not Healing

Our world seems to be full of those who condone and, in many cases, reward people who don't forgive. For example, a well-known rapper has a hit song full of venomous words spewed out at his mother, who allegedly mistreated him while he was a child. The lyrics show unforgiveness at its worst, for the rapper confesses to hating his mother, says he wishes she were dead, and then vows that his children (her grandchildren) will not even attend her funeral.

I believe in the freedom of expression—which this rapper obviously exercises—and I'm grateful for that freedom since it allows me to preach God's Word in this country without fear of persecution. This does not mean, however, that I agree with the rapper and support what he says. Regardless of how financially successful and popular he may be, God's Word is sure: Unforgiveness doesn't pay.

The message we hear over our airwaves or see on our TV screens is all too often one of revenge, not of forgiveness. Think of all the talk shows on TV these days in which a bitter son or daughter humiliates his or her parent in front of millions of Americans because of a past grievance. Sure, unforgiveness may appear trendy and popular, but those who harbor it slowly kill themselves from within. Hate never brings healing, just more hurt.

Think about it this way: When you don't forgive others their sins against you, *you* end up carrying the weight of their sins. In other words, when you become so consumed with wrongs committed against you that you think about them all the time, then *you* are the one who ends up feeling punished.

For the person who refuses to forgive, unforgiveness truly is a type of bondage. As the late Christian thinker and philosopher Lewis B. Smedes wrote, "To forgive is to set a prisoner free and discover the prisoner was you." [1] When you refuse to forgive, the person you're upset with isn't the only one who suffers. In fact you, as the unforgiver, suffers most—emotionally, spiritually, mentally, and relationally.

Not forgiving can even harm your physical health and well-being. When you refuse to forgive and choose instead to constantly dwell on evils done to you in the past, you perpetuate a hateful spirit that can literally wear your body down, leaving your immune system vulnerable to physical sicknesses of all sorts. To put it simply, a hateful, vengeful, unforgiving spirit is just plain bad for you.

> For the person who refuses to forgive, unforgiveness is a type of bondage.

Perhaps all this talk of hate and vengeance doesn't seem to apply to you. You're not singing hate-filled rap songs on the radio or exposing the faults of those who've hurt you on television. But are you stubbornly holding on to past grievances, no matter how small, and refusing to forgive? If so, then, essentially, you are behaving hatefully. While this may seem harsh, it's true. Merriam-Webster defines *hate* as "intense hostility and aversion usually deriving from fear, anger, or sense of injury." [2] Doesn't this express an unforgiving spirit? Think about it. Whenever we exercise a spirit of unforgiveness, we avoid others ("aver-

---

1. Lewis B. Smedes, "Forgiveness—The Power to Change the Past," used by permission, *Christianity Today*, January 7, 1983. <http://www.christianitytoday.com/ct/2002/149/55.0.html> (8 April, 2003)
2. *Merriam-Webster's Collegiate Dictionary*, Electronic Edition, Version 1.1, s.v. "hate."

sion") because of the anger or hurt pride that their actions have caused.

I'll admit that some grievances are so painful and deep that to even *think* about forgiving seems unbearable. In recent years, for instance, a major controversy over the sexual misconduct of priests with children from their parishes has surfaced. Undoubtedly, what these priests did was extremely painful for those children and families of those involved. Each of these priests has sinned, breaking not only the laws of men, but also God's law. These men have done wrong, and they deserve complete punishment for their crimes.

In situations such as this, it's easy to make excuses for not forgiving. "What they did was unforgivable!" we say, and we reason that it's okay not to forgive in such an extreme situation as this one.

But would Jesus agree with such a mind-set? Would He command forgiveness for some situations, but not for others? Did Jesus ever say, "Forgive your brother seventy times seven...except in cases of rape, murder, molestation, and abuse"? No. He simply commanded us to forgive, no matter what the situation was or who the offender is. Forgive. Period. No ifs, ands, or buts.

I admit, this is a tough pill to swallow, but isn't much of Christianity? God's ways are not man's ways, and we'll often find ourselves having to do things—like forgive the "unforgivable"—that are downright difficult. But their high level of difficulty doesn't mean we should do them any less. In fact, if we find that the decisions we're making are difficult, that's a pretty sure sign that we're on the right track.

*Enter by the narrow gate; for wide is the gate and broad is the way that leads to destruction, and there are many who go in by it. Because narrow is the*

*gate and difficult is the way which leads to life, and
there are few who find it.*          (Matthew 7:13–14)

No matter how difficult the process is, however, we can
be certain that God's ways are the best ways. Even when forgiving is tough, it is the path by which God will bring true
healing to our lives. No matter what the crime against you is,
holding on in hateful unforgiveness will only perpetuate the
pain, making you more and more of a prisoner. Remember,
"To forgive is to set a prisoner free and discover the prisoner
was you." [3] Will you remain a prisoner, or will you be set free
today? You must settle this question if you hope to maintain
the solid foundation upon which you have begun to build.

---

3. Lewis B. Smedes, "Forgiveness—The Power to Change the Past,"
used by permission, *Christianity Today,* January 7, 1983. <http://
www.christianitytoday.com/ct/2002/149/55.0.html> (8 April, 2003)

# Part IV

Learning from the
Three Little Pigs

# Introduction

*At that time the disciples came to Jesus, saying, "Who then is greatest in the kingdom of heaven?" Then Jesus called a little child to Him, set him in the midst of them, and said, "Assuredly, I say to you, unless you are converted and become as little children, you will by no means enter the kingdom of heaven. Therefore whoever humbles himself as this little child is the greatest in the kingdom of heaven. Whoever receives one little child like this in My name receives Me."*
—Matthew 18:1–5

We have a lot to learn from children. Aside from their nose-picking tendencies, their occasional affinity for kicking and biting, and their frequent confusion about which things are and are not appropriate to discuss in public, kids really do have a lot to teach us. Adults wanting to learn more about how to love unconditionally, how to forgive and forget, or even how to loosen up and just have fun whenever life gets stressful would be wise to spend a day or two studying children.

As Jesus taught in Matthew, we can even learn about faith from children. Jesus calls us to *"become as little children"* by humbling ourselves and by earnestly and unwaveringly trusting in Him. You've probably heard the expression "faith like a child," and here's where it comes from. Children have an ability to trust that many adults simply do not have because of walls they've built to protect themselves from broken promises and broken trusts.

But it's not just children who have something to teach us; children's literature holds invaluable lessons, too. Even as an adult I have enjoyed reading children's Bibles. The simple text and illustrated pages help me to visualize and to appreciate many Scripture stories that I've previously just breezed through. Reading through a child's eye opens up all kinds of new lessons.

We can even learn from traditional children's stories and fairy tales, such as "The Three Little Pigs." The story is a simple one, but it contains such great truths about the importance of building a solid foundation that I found it necessary to include the story here. I hope that this fresh, childlike look at what it means to lay a solid foundation will clarify and reinforce many of the principles discussed throughout this book.

Within this story we find what I like to call "the psychology of the three pigs." Each pig has his own unique character and mind-set, which are revealed in the choices that he makes. When we carefully consider each pig's frame of mind, we can better understand—and analyze the effectiveness of—the many different approaches that people take toward foundation-laying in their lives.

You're probably familiar with the story. It begins, "Once upon a time there were three little pigs, who left home to seek their fortune." [1] As we'll see in the following chapters,

1. From "Kid's Zone" on Mansfield/Richland County Public Library Webpage. <http://www.mrcpl.lib.oh.us/Children/KidZone.htm> (9 April, 2003)

the fairy tale then follows each pig through his house-building venture. Each pig picks a different material—straw, sticks, or bricks—for building his house, and each one faces different results, depending on his building materials. This reminds me of a Bible passage in which Paul discussed the importance of picking good materials for the foundations of our lives:

> *For no one can lay any foundation other than the one already laid, which is Jesus Christ. If any man builds on this foundation using gold, silver, costly stones, wood, hay or straw, his work will be shown for what it is, because the Day will bring it to light. It will be revealed with fire, and the fire will test the quality of each man's work. If what he has built survives, he will receive his reward. If it is burned up, he will suffer loss; he himself will be saved, but only as one escaping through the flames.*
> (1 Corinthians 3:11–15 NIV)

Paul's words remind us that Christ is our ultimate foundation. As we build upon this foundation, however, we must be careful that we pick the right materials. Will we use gold and silver? Stone and wood? Hay and straw? Whatever we pick will be tested by fire at the Lord's return—just as the little pigs' houses were tested by the wolf's "huffing and puffing"—so we'd better be certain that our building decisions have been wise.

Can your foundation stand the flames?

# Chapter Thirteen
# Pig Number One:
# The Straw Mentality

---

The first pig met a straw salesman on the road and immediately bought some straw. He then found an empty lot and set to work fashioning himself a house. In no time at all, the pig finished building his house, which he made entirely out of straw. The house was cute, but it certainly didn't look sturdy.

Soon enough, the house's stability was tested. A wolf came by and asked the little pig to let him into the house with the intent of eating him. The pig, fearful for his life, refused. The wolf, angered at the pig's refusal and intent on getting into the house in some way or another, began huffing and puffing until he blew the house down. (At this point, some fairy tales say the pig narrowly escaped, while others say he was eaten. Regardless of the outcome, however, I think you'd agree with me that neither one is ideal.)

This first little pig, like many people in our world today, suffered from what I like to call "the straw mentality." A person (or even a pig, for that matter) with this mind-set ignores the importance of foundation-laying and seeks instead to find as many shortcuts as possible. Speed is king (and ease is queen) for those who have the straw mentality.

Let's take a closer look at this first pig's building material. What exactly is straw? Straw consists of the hollow stalks left after ripened grains (wheat, rice, or oats, for example) have been harvested. Straw has been used for packing, for making beds, and even for fashioning hats that keep the sun out, but very seldom will you see a house made out of straw. If nothing else was available, a straw house could probably suffice for a short season, but it certainly would not survive very long. Imagine what would happen if a gentle breeze came along, much less a huge gust of wind! The person who uses straw is doomed to a life of apprehension and fearfulness as he continually wonders, "Will this storm be the one to knock me down?"

> The straw mentality ignores the importance of foundations in favor of shortcuts.

## Storms Are Inevitable

Those with straw mentalities are often on their knees, trying to pray the storms away. But contrary to some popular teachings, storms are sure to come into any person's life. Think about storms in the natural world. Even the most temperate, cloudless, sunny places on earth go through their seasons of intense storms and bad weather. We must face the reality that storms are bound to come in life.

In fact, the person who prays for "no storms" is immature and unwise in his request, for it is through such storms that God brings some of His greatest blessings. God strengthens us through these storms, and some lessons in life can only be learned through storms. *"My brethren, count it all joy when you fall into various trials, knowing that the testing of your faith produces patience. But let patience have its perfect work, that you may be perfect and complete, lacking nothing"* (James 1:2–4). As James reminded us, storms produce patience in our lives, and patience moves our characters closer and closer toward the perfection and completion that God desires for us.

Unfortunately, the person with a straw mentality misses out on such character-building, for he doesn't even have the appropriate foundation to withstand storms when they come. Instead of growing in wisdom and strength after each storm comes along, the person with a straw mentality must turn his attention toward clearing the ruins of his crumbled house and building it up again. The person with a straw mentality has no time for "growing up" in wisdom because he must spend all his time "cleaning up" his fallen house, and that is only in the best of cases. Sometimes the straw house is destroyed completely past the point of recovery. It is then that these people who live "for the moment"—never planning, never saving, and never reaping anything of lasting value—finally die "in a moment."

> The person with a straw mentality lacks character, for he doesn't have the foundation to withstand storms when they come.

## Do You Know Any Straw Men?

Since the straw mentality looks for quick fixes and easy results, those who adhere to it usually despise long-term plans. In the financial realm, they seldom own anything of real value since they buy impulsively. They never invest because they think waiting for a return just takes too long. They are impatient and want immediate outcomes. If they put money into something today, they want it doubled by tomorrow. Unfortunately, life doesn't work this way, and so those with a straw mentality are ill-equipped to handle day-to-day decisions, much less adversities when they strike.

Maybe you've encountered the straw mentality in churches you've visited or been a part of. It's found in those who love hearing about huge financial returns in exchange for one sizeable offering but hate to hear their pastor teach financial management skills and restricting spending habits. And they're certainly not interested in waiting around for compounded interest to take effect; they simply can't stand the thought of long-term commitment and planning, even though it will increase their investment tremendously.

People with the straw mentality live lives of constant defeat because they use the wrong building materials in their haste to get things done. With their straw, they build what may appear to be a picture-perfect home, but it seldom lasts for long. Are you seeking shortcuts and quick fixes at all costs, even to the point of using straw to build your home? Or are you willing to take the time necessary to build a lasting solid foundation?

# Chapter Fourteen
# Pig Number Two:
# The Stick Mentality

---

T he second pig met a stick salesman and, you guessed it, bought a bunch of sticks. Like his brother before him, he set off to find a lot and quickly started constructing his new home. What resulted was another cute house with questionable stability.

Although the stick house took a little bit longer to build than the straw house, and even though the sticks were a tad stronger than the straw used on the other house, the second pig's house was still not very strong. The stick house got its first test of stability just hours after it was built. The same hungry wolf dropped by, politely requested entrance into the house, and then proceeded to blow the house down when the pig refused to let him in. Needless to say, this house failed the stability test, just as the straw house had.

## Learning from Others

Whenever I hear this story, I have to ask myself why the second pig didn't learn from his brother's mistakes. If a mean old wolf had chased away (or killed) my brother, and I was building a house on the same street, I would be pretty careful about how I built my house. A stick home just wouldn't do it for me. In a word, I'd describe this second pig as "foolish."

Now, maybe you're saying here, "This is just a children's story. Nobody in real life would be that foolish." But is that really true? How many times have we heard of people dying in auto accidents because they weren't wearing their seat belts, even though they'd driven past signs every day reminding them of how seat belts had saved many lives? Or what about that time you had to stand by and watch your closest friend as he or she stubbornly made the same relationship mistakes you fell into just a year before? If you examine your life, I'm sure you'll encounter your own examples. We've all had those times when we've forged ahead in foolishness, despite the advice of others who had already made the same mistake we were about to make. At times, we are much like young children who insist on touching the stove, even though Mom has just said, "Don't touch that or you'll get burned." This is one example where childlike behavior is not desirable!

> Some people insist on learning the hard way, like the toddler who touches the stove after his mother's warning.

So many people insist on learning things the hard way, just like the toddler who touches the stove after his mother's warning. Why is this? Some would label such behavior as stubborn pride, while others would call it mere curiosity. Whatever you call it though, the results are almost always tragic. When it comes to the spiritual realm, the results can even be fatal: *"The wages of sin is death"* (Romans 6:23).

Even though we know Romans 6:23 to be true, we often choose slave wages over God's free gift of abundant life when the enemy of our souls confronts us with sinful propositions. To try to make sense out of such conduct is usually useless. It's hard to figure out why we make the foolish choices we do, and even harder to rationalize the stubbornness of certain people who just won't heed advice. I have lived long enough to realize that some people will live how they want to, no matter how serious the risks or how adamant the warnings from those around them.

But for those who do want to make wise decisions and thus avoid the path of pig number two, there's an old adage that's good to keep in mind. The expression, which says, "Experience is a great teacher," is often interpreted as referring to our own experiences. For example, if I ran out of gas last week because I wasn't paying attention to my gas gauge, then I know *from experience* to pay more attention in the future. Learning from our own experiences is a good thing, but we can extend this principle even further: *Learn from other people's experiences.* When it comes to learning the difficult lessons in life, learn them as much as possible from someone who's already "been there, done that." If you don't have to go through it yourself, then don't. Let the past failures and struggles of those around you serve as reminders of what paths you should avoid. If you just saw your neighbor's house fall down, please don't make your house the exact same way.

## An Example from God's Word

In the story of Joshua and his predecessor Moses, the Bible gives an excellent example of how we can learn from the mistakes of others. Moses was a great man of

God whom the Lord used to deliver the children of Israel out of Egypt. Much of his life was centered around leading God's people to the Promised Land, and for the most part he was faithful in carrying out all that the Lord commanded him. Because of one emotionally charged bad decision, however, Moses was prevented from seeing the Promised Land:

> Then the LORD spoke to Moses, saying, "Take the rod; you and your brother Aaron gather the congregation together. Speak to the rock before their eyes, and it will yield its water; thus you shall bring water for them out of the rock, and give drink to the congregation and their animals." So Moses took the rod from before the LORD as He commanded him. And Moses and Aaron gathered the assembly together before the rock; and he said to them, "Hear now, you rebels! Must we bring water for you out of this rock?" Then Moses lifted his hand and struck the rock twice with his rod; and water came out abundantly, and the congregation and their animals drank. Then the LORD spoke to Moses and Aaron, "Because you did not believe Me, to hallow Me in the eyes of the children of Israel, therefore you shall not bring this assembly into the land which I have given them."
>
> (Numbers 20:7–12)

Did you catch what Moses did? The Lord commanded Moses to speak to the rock and Moses disobeyed by striking the rock. Now, this may not seem like a big deal at first glance, but it really was. By striking the rock instead of speaking to it, Moses tried to "steal the show" from God and get praises from the people for himself. God would not tolerate such disobedience, however, and He punished Moses by promising that Moses would not be the one to lead God's people into the Promised Land. In fact, Moses would die before Israel entered the Promised Land.

Joshua, Moses' understudy, was the man God chose to lead His people into Canaan. Now Joshua could have chosen to follow the same path as his mentor by disregarding God's commands in the same way that Moses had, but he didn't. Instead, Joshua wisely chose to learn from Moses' life lesson. Because he was able to observe another man's mistake, he could avoid making that same blunder and thus escape the same punishment that Moses had received.

> We would love to dwell on our successes, but we must also learn to glean understanding from the failures.

Examples such as these abound, both inside and outside of Scripture. We can learn much as we revisit history's battles—especially those we didn't win. Of course we would love to dwell on the victories and successes, but that, unfortunately, will not always lead us on the pathway of wisdom for tomorrow. We must learn to glean understanding from the failures as well as the successes.

Every dip in the stock market can serve as a learning experience for those who are preparing to invest in the future. Every failed fad diet can help the new dieter know what pitfalls to avoid. And every collapsed building can provide important information for architects and construction workers seeking to make stronger, safer, and sounder structures.

## A Little Better...but Not Quite Enough

Who knows? Maybe little pig number two thought he *was* learning from his straw-mentality brother. "Hey," he might have said, "Straw didn't work for my brother, so I'll try something stronger. How about sticks?" And so he proceeded to do what he thought was wise, only to be knocked down (literally) in the end.

The problem with pig number two was that he didn't upgrade his materials enough. Instead of moving on to unquestionably stronger materials, he settled for something just a little bit stronger. This stick mentality is as dangerous and deadly as the straw mentality.

While the person with a straw mentality tries to get by with the bare minimum, those with the stick mentality try to do just a little bit more, but it's never quite enough. These are the people who do not want to associate with the "losers" (who have a straw mentality) but they still won't do what it takes to create a winner's edge. People of the stick mentality don't mind being average. As long as they are just slightly better than the losers, they think they're fine. Unfortunately, those with a stick mentality face the same fate as those with a straw mentality: eventual destruction.

# Going Beyond All Perceived Limitations

God has not called us to be limited by the stick mentality. He has called us instead to move beyond the status quo as we pursue excellence. *"And whatever you do, do it heartily, as to the Lord and not to men, knowing that from the Lord you will receive the reward of the inheritance; for you serve the Lord Christ"* (Colossians 3:23–24).

We are made in the image of the One who created us and He calls us to work hard at all we do, so that we may glorify His name.

Unfortunately, not everyone sees things this way. In spiritual circles, for instance, I have personally witnessed unfair treatment toward women in ministry, and I'm pleased whenever I discover women who are overcoming the limitations that many men in positions of authority have placed on them. There are women pastors, both here in our country and abroad, who are sharing the Gospel of Christ with thousands of people, leading great congregations, and making their communities better places to live and work. I am grateful for their accomplishments.

Unfortunately, these relatively few women are only a small portion of the many women who have been called into active service for the Lord. Sadly, a great number of women have allowed man-made traditions to stifle God's gift of ministry within them. This mental posture deeply grieves God. I believe that He calls us to go beyond all perceived limitations. Whatever your limitation seems to be, God has allowed it for a purpose. That purpose is not to deter or discourage you, but rather to bring glory to His name as He works in you to march around that limitation. Every challenge and struggle that has been placed in your life is an opportunity for advancement, not an excuse to stay where you are or turn back in fear.

During Jacob's struggle with the angel of the Lord, his hip was severely disjointed:

> *And he arose that night and took his two wives, his two female servants, and his eleven sons, and crossed over the ford of Jabbok. He took them, sent them over the brook, and sent over what he had. Then Jacob was left alone; and a Man wrestled with him until the breaking of day. Now when He saw that He did not prevail against him, He touched the socket of his hip; and the socket of Jacob's hip was out of joint as He wrestled with him. And He said, "Let Me go, for the day breaks." But he said, "I will not let You go unless You bless*

*me!" So He said to him, "What is your name?"
He said, "Jacob." And He said, "Your name shall
no longer be called Jacob, but Israel; for you have
struggled with God and with men, and have pre-
vailed." Then Jacob asked, saying, "Tell me Your
name, I pray." And He said, "Why is it that you
ask about My name?" And He blessed him there.
And Jacob called the name of the place Peniel:
"For I have seen God face to face, and my life
is preserved." Just as he crossed over Penuel
the sun rose on him, and he limped on his hip.*
(Genesis 32:22–31)

Obviously, Jacob experienced great pain because of
this disability. He very easily could have opted for the stick
mentality, which would have been the easy way out. He
could have said, "Well, at least I had an encounter with
the Lord. Most people never come this close to having
angelic experiences in their lives, and so I'm satisfied with
what just happened. That should be enough. I don't need
a blessing."

Jacob didn't choose this easy way out, though. Instead,
he pressed on. "I'm already wounded," he said, in essence,
"so I may as well keep moving. If I die, then I die. If I
live, then I will have the blessing. I will keep wrestling
until I receive the blessing I seek." The blessing was more
important to Jacob than the short-term pain he had to go
through to get it. He pressed on, choosing not to simply
"settle" for something good when he could taste something even better.

The stick mentality is happy to weigh in as average. A
person with this mind-set is happy for a "C" even though
God is calling him or her to earn an "A." Has the stick
mentality surfaced in your life? Are you content with the

status quo when God is calling you to excellence? It is my prayer that as you build your solid foundation, you will choose only the best materials, never settling for measly sticks.

# Chapter Fifteen
# Pig Number Three:
# The Brick Mentality

---

The third little pig sought out a brick salesman and bought a bunch of bricks. (Notice how he *sought out* the brick salesman, unlike his brothers who just happened upon some street vendors. This third little pig understood the importance of being intentional.) After securing his bricks in his cart, he set off to the lot he'd purchased a few weeks before and started working to construct his new home.

This house took a lot longer to build than his brothers' houses, but what resulted was not only beautiful but also strong and sturdy. The wolf stopped by this house, too, but what he found there was quite different from what he had found at the other two homes. This one would not budge.

## Formula for Stability

What set this pig apart from his brothers? Why was he able to succeed when his brothers failed horribly? I think you know the answer. He was willing to exert the extra effort necessary to ensure success, and that's why his house was found standing in the end. Unlike his straw-mentality brother, pig number three didn't want any shortcuts. He wouldn't settle for mediocre materials like his stick-mentality brother, either. Instead, he sharpened his skills, supplied his fair share, and then sat back to taste his sweet success. This pig aimed for perfection, and in aiming, he attained it.

## Sharpening Your Skills

In addition to using sturdy, stable materials that had passed the test of time, this pig had know-how, or knowledge. In order to build a brick house, a person first needs some masonry skills.

Pig number three had knowledge and skills that didn't come naturally. He had to work for them. Masonry is hard work, and it requires an intricate understanding of the materials and the process itself. Most likely he had worked long hard hours shadowing another mason before he mastered this skill. This pig was willing to invest time and energy into his endeavor.

## Supplying Your Fair Share

Not only did pig number three invest in solid materials and bring expert skills to this building project; he also came prepared with the equipment and supplies that he knew he'd need. The story doesn't say that the pig bought the lime, the mortar, the sand, and the trowel from the brick salesman. No! He already had these things. The pig knew, going into his venture, all that he would need, and he made sure ahead of time to bring the bulk of the materials with him. When he entered his new neighborhood, he only needed one final material to make his project complete, and that was the bricks.

What does this mean for us in our foundation-laying endeavors? It means that we, too, must come prepared. In the work world, for instance, it means that every person involved in a business venture must be willing to invest in that venture. They all need to put forth time and money—or else it's too easy to walk away if things turn sour. If each one has his own money, time, and materials tied up in a project, however, they'll be linked to that project and less likely to just give up.

When we began receiving contributions from people who wanted to sow into our vision and help build The First Cathedral, we already had some funds on hand that we had been saving long before we even purchased the property. If we had not had any money to contribute to our vision, it might never have come to fruition. The same is true in business. If you have a remarkable business plan, yet you have no capital at all reserved for that business, you probably won't find anyone who's willing to invest in your dream. People enjoy investing in dreams into which an investment has already been made.

> People enjoy investing in dreams into which an investment has already been made.

I use this principle whenever I try to decide which ministries to financially support. God has burdened me to be a sower of seeds, and I look, with great enthusiasm, for opportunities to financially bless ministries that are on the move for God. If a church is building a new worship facility, buying equipment to make the gospel message more accessible, or starting up a new congregation, I want to join with them in making the dream become a reality. I'm hesitant, however, when there appears to be little or no investment on that church's part.

## Seeing the Success

When we invest, others are willing to join in on the investment. Just as I'm happy to support a church that's already put forth its fair share, others will be willing to help you in your endeavors when you've already done your part.

Even more wonderful is this truth: When you take one step, God takes two. In other words, when you invest in a project—whether it be through time, money, prayer, or effort—God brings great returns. If you don't put anything into it, though, there's nothing for God to work with or expand upon. While it's true that God could easily do the project without us or our supplies—for He created the heavens and the earth by Himself out of nothing!—this is not the way He chooses to work today.

Think about Noah. Did God just drop an ark out of heaven for this man of God to use? No. He chose to let mankind be a crucial part of his plan by requiring Noah to invest the time, energy, work, and tears necessary to build this boat.

Or consider another ark—the ark of the covenant—and the tabernacle that housed it. God had special requirements for every nook and cranny of his structure, including specifics on which fabrics, woods, gems, and metals were to be used, as well as detailed measurements for every section of the tabernacle from the entranceway to the Holy of Holies. Look at the instructions He gave to Moses on Mt. Sinai:

> *And let them make Me a sanctuary, that I may dwell among them. According to all that I show you, that is, the pattern of the tabernacle and the pattern of all its furnishings, just so you shall make it.*
> (Exodus 25:8–9)

It's pretty clear from this passage that God wanted His people to be part of His plan. God provided the pattern, but it was the people who did the building. This was no easy project, and perhaps it would have been simpler if God had just built it Himself. There's no doubt He could have done so if He wanted to. But again, this was not how He chose to work. He desired for mankind to be part of the working out of His plan, and so He provided avenues for every man and woman to be involved—from the carpenters, to the jewelers, to the blacksmiths, to the seamstresses. God wanted all of Israel to be involved, and *then* He would bless the work of their hands.

So often in the church I see a *laissez-faire* or "let it be" attitude when it comes to furthering the kingdom of God. This saddens me, as I'm sure it does our Lord. Prayer is important, but we must never use it as a substitute for the actions God is also calling us to take. He works *through* us to further His kingdom as we vow to work *for* Him.

> God works through us to further His kingdom as we vow to work for Him.

# Chapter Sixteen
# A Wolf's Mind: The Enemy Mentality

So far we've looked at the psychologies of the three little pigs, but there is a fourth psychology here to consider, that of the wolf. It would be unfair to deal with the mentalities of the three little pigs and not give equal attention to the wolf. Much like the wolf's goal in the fairy tale to catch and eat the three pigs, a wolf's goal in the Christian's life is to scatter Christ's sheep and devour them.

## A Breakdown of the Big Bad Wolf

In the midst of wolf attacks, Scripture tells us that our Good Shepherd, Jesus Christ, protects us:

*I am the good shepherd. The good shepherd gives His life for the sheep. But a hireling, he who is not the shepherd, one who does not own the sheep, sees the wolf coming and leaves the sheep and flees; and the wolf catches the sheep and scatters them.*
(John 10:11–12)

We should still take steps to understand the wolf, however, so we can avoid him when he comes. Wolves always seek out the weakest, the babies, in a group. They separate these weak ones from the rest of the sheep, making them more vulnerable, and then they attack. Scripture exhorts us to grow spiritually so that we can avoid and escape such attacks. *"As newborn babes, desire the pure milk of the word, that you may grow"* (1 Peter 2:2).

To better understand this enemy, the wolf, we'll take a look at his purpose, his prey, and his plan.

## The Wolf's Purpose

Who is this wolf? The ultimate wolf is Satan, who tries to snatch us from Christ. Even though Satan is powerful, he is far less powerful than our Creator God, and we can take comfort in the fact that absolutely nothing can separate us from Christ:

> *Who shall separate us from the love of Christ? Shall tribulation, or distress, or persecution, or famine, or nakedness, or peril, or sword?...For I am persuaded that neither death nor life, nor angels nor principalities nor powers, nor things present nor things to come, nor height nor depth, nor any other created thing, shall be able to separate us from the love of God which is in Christ Jesus our Lord.*
> (Romans 8:35, 38–39)

The Bible speaks of other wolves, too. At one point, Jesus described false prophets as wolves. The goal of such prophets is to deceptively pull God's children away from God and His Word.

> *Beware of false prophets, who come to you in sheep's clothing, but inwardly they are ravenous wolves.* (Matthew 7:15)

## His Prey

As we saw before, wolves go after the uninitiated, those who haven't yet absorbed the truths of God's Word. In the church, wolves always seek out those who are new to the faith. They are always on the lookout for opportunities to snatch them away and devour them.

Newborn babies have no sense of who is and who is not a proper guardian. They embrace anyone who will feed them, change their diapers, and make them feel comfortable. Spiritual newborns are a perfect target for wolves, because they are open to help from anyone who will provide it, whether it is good help or not.

Children can be prime targets, too. Because they are young and still learning about the world around them, children believe almost anything. Spiritual children are good targets for wolves because they still have much to learn about Christ and His ways and may therefore accept what they hear more readily. When wolves come to churches, they don't usually go after the spiritual mothers, the deacons, or the teachers in the church. They go after the simple, those with limited knowledge and experience.

## His Plan

A wolf's plan of attack always involves trickery, deceit, and sneakiness. Think back to the story of the three little pigs. The wolf pretended to be a friend to the pigs by politely requesting entrance into their homes.

Wolves in the Christian life are very much the same. Look again at Matthew 7:15: *"Beware of false prophets, who come to you in sheep's clothing, but inwardly they are ravenous wolves."* According to this verse, wolves will go so far as to disguise themselves as sheep so that they can gain easy access to the "sheep pen," or the church.

This is pretty scary stuff, since it means the enemy may very well be among us. How do we protect ourselves from an enemy who's standing on our very own ground?

# Keeping the Sheep Safe

Fortunately, the outlook isn't helpless. These ferocious infiltrators *can* be defeated. Why else would Jesus tell us to *"Beware"*? The fact that He told us to be careful lets us know that these wolves can in fact be spotted, avoided, and even chased off.

## Spotting the Wolf

How will we recognize wolves when they enter our lives? Clearly it won't be an easy task since Jesus told us that they disguise themselves as sheep. It can be done, however. Look at Matthew 7:16–20:

> *You will know them by their fruits. Do men gather grapes from thornbushes or figs from thistles? Even so, every good tree bears good fruit, but a bad tree bears bad fruit. A good tree cannot bear bad fruit, nor can a bad tree bear good fruit. Every tree that does not bear good fruit is cut down and thrown into the fire. Therefore by their fruits you will know them.*
> (Matthew 7:16–20)

Jesus said here that we will be able to recognize wolves by their fruit. In other words, as we spend time with them, their actions, aims, and attitudes will clarify for us whether they are from the Lord or not.

Here, during this fruit inspection stage, is where God's Word comes in. It is crucial that we be familiar with what a Christian looks like *according to the Bible*. Sometimes in the church we come up with our own litmus tests for judging whether or not someone is a Christian. "Well," we say, "he wears Christian T-shirts, listens to gospel music, and has a Jesus fish on his car's bumper. He must be a Christian!" Such thinking is totally false. Where in the Bible does God say that listening to Christian music makes a person a Christian? Nowhere!

Instead, we must use biblical standards and principles. For instance, does this person demonstrate *"love, joy, peace, longsuffering, kindness, goodness, faithfulness, gentleness, self-control"* (Galatians 5:22–23). Does he show a desire for the furtherance of God's kingdom, or does he seek only after his own glory and advancement? It is in thoughtfully asking and answering questions such as these that we can pinpoint wolves whenever they enter into our lives.

> Once you have identified the wolf, limit your contact and communication with him or her.

## Avoiding the Wolf

Once you've identified a wolf, it's your job to limit your contact and communication with him or her. Like pig number three, we need to be wise in whom we give access to our lives.

Nowadays, most people understand the need to secure their houses properly. They invest in fancy dead bolts, heavy-duty doors, and even security alarm systems. It is not easy to get into a house unless you've been welcomed inside first. We should treat our lives the same way. Not just anyone should have access to your time, your heart, and your thoughts. There are some people who I believe are assigned by hell to totally undermine your progress in life. These people are not intended to bless you but rather distract you from your real purpose. You need to avoid such people at all costs. We are not to welcome wolves into our lives or try to be "buddy-buddy" with them. Instead, the Lord tells us to cut ties with them.

Scripture is filled with verses that emphasize the importance of choosing carefully whom we hang out with. Here are just a few:

> *Do not be unequally yoked together with unbelievers. For what fellowship has righteousness with lawlessness? And what communion has light with darkness?* (2 Corinthians 6:14)

> *Do not be deceived: "Evil company corrupts good habits."* (1 Corinthians 15:33)

> *He who walks with wise men will be wise, but the companion of fools will be destroyed.* (Proverbs 13:20)

> *And have no fellowship with the unfruitful works of darkness, but rather expose them.* (Ephesians 5:11)

> *And if anyone does not obey our word in this epistle, note that person and do not keep company with him, that he may be ashamed. Yet do not count him as an enemy, but admonish him as a brother.* (2 Thessalonians 3:14–15)

We are not to keep close company with those whose lives are not in line with the Lord. A wolf—who tries to scatter the Lord's flock—would definitely fall into this category. Don't be friends with the enemy. When you spot a wolf, make a clean break, as soon as you can.

## Chasing the Wolf Away

When we spot a wolf, we need to break our interactions with him at all costs, but this doesn't mean we can't first outsmart him to get rid of him for good!

Since the wolf is wily, we need to be wily, too. Remember what Jesus said? *"Behold, I send you out as sheep in the midst of wolves. Therefore be wise as serpents and harmless as doves"* (Matthew 10:16).

Let's go back to the little pig story for a bit. What happened when the wolf tried to blow the brick house down? It didn't move one inch. Do you know what happened at this point? The wolf was certainly foiled and befuddled, but unfortunately he didn't give up. Instead, he turned back to the drawing board to concoct another plan for snagging that pig. "If I can't get into the house," he thought, "I'll just have to get the pig out of the house."

The wolf then ended up turning to trickery to get the pig to come out. "Come join me at Farmer Smith's tomorrow evening to pick turnips, fresh from the garden!" he said. And then, "How about joining me for some apple-picking tomorrow!" And finally, "Let's go to the fair tomorrow afternoon!" The pig, using some cunning of his own, was wise in his responses. At a glance it seems that he let his guard down, for he consented to join the wolf for every single one of these events. The truth, though, is that the pig ended up using some wiles of his own.

Pig number three knew that timing was everything, and he used this to his advantage. Even though the pig accepted the wolf's offers, he accepted them on his own terms and with his own timing, not when and how the wolf wanted things to be done. Pig number three went to every one of these events—turnip-picking, apple-picking, and the fair—but for each one he showed up an hour earlier than the wolf. By the time the wolf was ready to go, the pig was already finished! In the end, the pig was able to eat the food and enjoy the fair simply because he understood the importance of timing.

This pig used his smarts and shrewdness to always stay one step ahead of the wolf. In the end, these smarts paid off when Mr. Wolf fell right into a pot of boiling water that the pig had prepared for him. By being wily and quick-thinking, pig number three was able not only to protect himself but also to expose the wolf's wicked schemes and dispose of him in the end.

Are you taking steps to identify, avoid, and even chase away the wolves in your life? Or are you silently standing by as they huff, puff, and blow your straw home down? Only those who have built a solid foundation can move on to fight off the wolves.

# Part V

# Remembering the Fundamentals: Christ and the Church

## Chapter Seventeen
# Getting Back to Basics: Jesus Is Our Rock

A s we're laying any solid foundation in our lives, it's often easy to forget who *the* Foundation is—Jesus Christ. This is a pitfall that we must be aware of and take steps to avoid, for anything without Christ at its center is meaningless and in vain.

If you're laying a financial foundation, for instance, who cares how many books, manuals, and pamphlets you read about saving and investing? If you end up forgetting whose glory it should be for, it's all for nothing. As nineteenth-century Christian missionary C. T. Studd once said, "Only one life, it will soon be past. Only what's done for Christ will last." [1]

Even if you've already established Christ as the foundation of your life by accepting His gift of salvation, it's easy to let other foundations replace Him in your mind—the foundations of family, career, church, friends, or other distractions.

1. Oneliners and Proverbs. <http://www.oneliners-and-proverbs.com/O_o.html> (9 April, 2003)

We're all susceptible to this, and for this reason it's important that we intentionally and regularly remind ourselves who our Foundation is.

# Who Is This Rock?

I personally get very annoyed when people speak to me in vague terminology, so I want to make sure that I am direct and to the point here. Before we launch into a discussion of how to stay grounded in our Foundation, I want to take time to establish exactly whom I'm talking about when I refer to Jesus Christ.

Unfortunately, talking about God and the real biblical Jesus is not very popular these days, unless it's in the context of a very generic, watered-down Gospel. One popular method of contemporary metaphysics seeks to blend concepts from all faiths and religions together into a sort of spiritual potpourri. They start with Jesus as a base, throw in a little bit of Buddha, add a dash of Confucius, and top it off with some New Age thinking. But this is not what I mean when I talk about God. Christianity is not a hodgepodge of principles drawn from the best thinkers and teachers of all time. It is the story of Jesus Christ, God's Son, coming to earth to redeem sinners.

Many think of Jesus as just a great teacher and example for mankind. While it's true that His life on earth was filled with many great teachings and examples for us to follow, Jesus Christ was (and is) so much more than just a teacher and example. The Jesus Christ of whom I speak is God incarnate. He is the Word made flesh. In other words, He is God, come down to earth in the form of man! He is Emmanuel—God with us! This God is Alpha and Omega, the beginning and the end, the Creator of all. He is the God who breathed life into mankind and the God who delivers His chosen ones from death. He is Savior and Sanctifier, Great

Physician, Redeemer. This is the Lord of whom I speak, and He is the Foundation upon which every believer must build.

Talking about Jesus like this may not be popular, but who cares about what's popular if it's the right thing? Unfortunately, many people concern themselves so much with what's in vogue that they take the popular road at all costs, even if it's harmful. We see this in youth who try drugs and alcohol just to be cool. Such behavior is risky, and when it comes to issues of eternity, the stakes are even higher. Even if it's not "cool" to talk about God and His salvation, I still choose to do so, for this is an issue that has eternal consequences. It deserves to be discussed, whether it's popular or not.

After all, Jesus is our solid Rock. He is the foundation upon which all of Christianity rests, and therefore the foundation upon which each of our lives rests. Certainly we should talk about Him, study Him, and figure out how we can best stick close by His side.

Before we go much further, let's talk a little bit about rocks. Since Jesus is our Rock, shouldn't we understand some basics on the characteristics and qualities of rocks?

Rocks, which are made of minerals, are hard. In fact, they are among the hardest substances known to naturally exist on earth. When a person's character is likened to a rock, we mean that that person has amazing strength or stability. We can lean on a person who is "like a rock" because that person will remain a stable support for us, never budging. Rocks can even be seen as places of refuge and shelter since they are protective, blocking out wind, rain, and storm. When we say that Christ is the Rock, we are reminded that He is stable, sturdy, solid, unmoving, and unchanging. He is a shelter and a refuge for us in times of trial, and we know that we need never fear whenever we are leaning on Him.

# Keeping Close to the Rock

There's a familiar old hymn called "What a Friend We Have in Jesus" that many Christians have grown to love over the years. The hymn's lyrics hold profound spiritual lessons, one of which is beautifully captured in the last line of stanza one: "Oh, what peace we often forfeit, oh, what needless pain we bear, all because we do not carry everything to God in prayer." [1] With these words, the songwriter reminds us that so often our trials become ten, twenty, or even a hundred times worse simply because we do not turn to our Lord, our Rock, for refuge, comfort, and protection.

> Often, we pretend that we are solid rocks, even though "we are weak, but He is strong."

Joseph M. Scriven, the writer of this hymn's lyrics, was no stranger to trials, for he lost his fiancée to drowning the night before their wedding. Scriven, who wrote these words to comfort his mother during a serious illness she was battling, clearly understood firsthand the necessity of earnestly seeking after the Lord in times of trial.

Often, instead of seeking after the Lord in times of trial, we turn to ourselves first. We pretend that *we* are solid rocks, even though "[We] are weak, but He is strong," [2] as another popular song reminds us. We so quickly forget our recent failures and immediately try playing the part of self-savior, even though our track records suggest that that is not such a good idea.

In Matthew 6:31–32, Jesus admonished us not to be consumed with plans and preparations for providing for our physical needs. *"Therefore do not worry, saying, 'What shall we eat?' or 'What shall we drink?' or 'What shall we wear?' For*

1. <www.cyberhymnal.org/htm/w/a/wafwhij.htm> (15 April, 2003)
2. <http://www.cyberhymnal.org/htm/j/e/jesuslme.htm> (16 April, 2003)

*after all these things the Gentiles seek. For your heavenly Father knows that you need all these things."* Instead, we are to *"seek first"* His kingdom, for is only there that we will find anything of rock-solid, lasting worth. *"But seek first the kingdom of God and His righteousness, and all these things shall be added to you"* (Matthew 6:33).

Notice how Matthew 6:33 holds a promise. When we seek God's kingdom first, all the things that used to worry us—food, drink, clothes—need no longer be worries, for the Lord tends to them according to His perfect timing and will. *"But seek first the kingdom of God and His righteousness, **and all these things shall be added to you"** (emphasis added).

Does this mean that we are to seek God only during times of trial and worry? By no means! Seeking Him on a daily basis, whether we are struggling or not, is the only way to secure spiritual success and ensure that we are always glorifying Him. It is only as we seek Him continually—during the good and the bad—that we learn how solid a foundation our Jesus, the Rock, really is.

## When He Says "Move," Move

As we begin seeking the Lord regularly, we'll find ourselves being able to discern His leading in our lives. Along with this discernment comes the necessity to put that discernment into practice. We must learn to let every action be guided by His command. In other words, we need to learn how to 1) hear the Lord's voice, 2) do what He says, and 3) patiently sit still during those times that we don't hear Him.

I'm known for saying, "If the Lord didn't say 'do it,' then don't do it." After seeing or hearing about our newly built cathedral, people have said to me, "Bishop, I think it's time for our church to build a cathedral, too. I've been pastoring this church for twenty years now, and we're past due for a nice building of our own."

Trust me when I say that anyone with this desire to build has my blessing. No one but the Lord knows how much I would love to see more beauti-

> God's words to you will never contradict His Word.

ful church structures built around this country and around the world as the body of Christ takes charge and seizes possession of the land for the Lord. But you see, my desire and your desire are not the issue at all. You may have my blessing and consent to undertake a building project, but do you have God's? His blessing is the one that counts.

If God has not said to you, "Rise up and build," then don't do it just because someone else did. During my years as a pastor, I have seen countless people fail in ministry because of this mistake. Instead of doing what God told them to do, they pursued what was popular. This is a sure recipe for disappointment.

I see this mistake when it comes to relationships all the time. Scores of young people rush into marriage because all their friends are getting married, not because they're ready to tie the knot. Such marriages, which fail to seek and follow God's timing, often end in turmoil and heartache. Had these couples waited for God's "go-ahead" instead of acting on the approval of their friends, they could have avoided a lot of pain.

Being able to clearly hear and discern God's voice doesn't come naturally. It is a skill that the Holy Spirit cultivates in your heart and mind as you set aside time to seek God through prayer and His Word. Remember, God's words to you will *never* contradict His Word. Any instructions He gives will always be consistent and in step with Scripture. That is why it's so important to be in the Word on a regular basis.

Don't be afraid to carefully evaluate what you believe the Lord is telling you in order to make sure it really is from Him. This is what discernment is all about. He does not want us to go simply because we heard a voice say, "Go." Instead, He wants us to make sure that voice we're hearing really is His before we decide to obey it.

> *Beloved, do not believe every spirit, but test the spirits, whether they are of God; because many false prophets have gone out into the world. By this you know the Spirit of God: Every spirit that confesses that Jesus Christ has come in the flesh is of God, and every spirit that does not confess that Jesus Christ has come in the flesh is not of God.* (1 John 4:1–3)

Our Lord is a solid rock.

# Chapter Eighteen
# Mirroring Our Lord:
# A Church That's Rock-Solid

---

J ust as Christ is rock-solid, so too is His church. The Lord's church is so solid, strong, and stable that even Satan cannot overcome it, no matter how hard he tries.

Before we go any further, let's take a look at Matthew 16:18, where Jesus said, *"On this rock I will build My church, and the gates of Hades shall not prevail against it."* This verse deserves special attention, because many have taken it out of context and misinterpreted its meaning. Many believe that Jesus gave Peter special authority through this verse. In other words, they believe that Jesus was referring to Peter when He said *"this rock."* Is this what Jesus was really saying to Peter? Was Jesus saying that He would build *His* church— the one He bled and died for—upon someone else? This just doesn't make sense.

A careful look at the meaning of Peter's name helps us to more clearly understand exactly what this verse is saying.

According to *Strong's Exhaustive Concordance,* Peter's name comes from the Greek word *Petros,* meaning "a (piece of) rock." [1] Peter was merely a piece of rock, like a stone or a pebble. However, Jesus said He would build His church on a large, massive rock. When He said, *"on this rock I will build My church,"* he used the word, *petra,* meaning "a (mass of) rock." [2] Peter was merely a pebble, but Christ was going to build His church on a boulder.

What exactly is this boulder that Christ referred to? For the answer to this question, we need to go back a few verses. Look at Matthew 16:15–19:

> *He said to them, "But who do you say that I am?" Simon Peter answered and said, "You are the Christ, the Son of the living God." Jesus answered and said to him, "Blessed are you, Simon Bar-Jonah, for flesh and blood has not revealed this to you, but My Father who is in heaven. And I also say to you that you are Peter, and on this rock I will build My church, and the gates of Hades shall not prevail against it. And I will give you the keys of the kingdom of heaven, and whatever you bind on earth will be bound in heaven, and whatever you loose on earth will be loosed in heaven."*

The rock upon which Christ said He would build His church, was the confession that Peter gave in verse 16: *"You are the Christ, the Son of the living God."* It is upon the faith of believers that the Lord has built His church, and this is the rock to which Christ referred. Our faith is intricately interwoven with Jesus Christ, and so we can also consider the Lord Himself to be the Rock on which the church is built.

---

1. *Strong's Exhaustive Concordance* (Thomas Nelson Publishers), s.v. G#4074 "Petros."
2. Ibid., s.v. G#4073 "petra."

# The Church: A Basic Definition

Before we go much further, I want to clarify what we mean when we say "church," for there is often much confusion surrounding this term. We need to be confident that we know what the church *is* and what it *is not.*

## The Church Is Not a Building

First, the church is not a building. There is a children's rhyme, accompanied by hand motions, that goes like this: "Here is the church, here is the steeple; open the door and see all the people." During this little rhyme, a child pretends that his folded hands are the church building ("Here is the church"), his index fingers are the steeple ("here is the steeple"), and all his other fingers are the church attendees ("open the door and see all the people").

Unfortunately, adults often equate "church" with the church building, much as this rhyme does. Instead of saying, "I'm going to the church building," we say, "I'm going to the church." Perhaps this seems trivial, but the issue comes down to more than just a play on words. We must never succumb to the mind-set that places importance on a building rather than the people who gather in it. While a building is nice, the church does not need a building. The church, at its simplest, is God's people working together as one to obey God's rules, to glorify God in action and in deed, and to further God's kingdom. The solid Rock, Jesus Christ, has already been laid; no other construction is needed.

> The church is God's people working together to obey His rules, glorify Him, and further His kingdom.

# The Church Is More Than Local

If someone asked you, "What church do you attend?" what would your answer be? If someone then asked you, "What church do you belong to?" would your answer be the same? In all honesty, your responses to these two questions should not be identical. Let me explain.

When someone asks, "What church do you attend?" they want to know which local congregation you're a part of. Do you go to the Church of Christ on Ninth Street, the Assembly of God on Main, or the Reformed Baptist on Wilson Avenue? A person who asks you this question wants to know which group of local believers you regularly meet with for worship, service, and fellowship.

When someone asks you the second question—"Which church do you belong to?"—they may think they're asking you about which local body you attend, but I'd like to point out that these questions really are quite different. You see, the answer to "Which church do you belong to?" should be "Jesus Christ's church." The church is not limited to one location. It is made up of believers from all over the world, and the thing that binds them together is not the building they're in, the songs they sing, the Bible version they use, or the type of cracker they pass out at communion. None of these things defines the church. What does define the church is the Lord who saved her, who is sanctifying her now, and who will one day take her to her eternal home.

> The church is the Lord's bride. He seeks after us, just as a man woos the woman he loves.

# The Church: Standing at the End

No matter what happens in this world, one thing is sure—God's church isn't going anywhere. There have been countless attempts throughout history to destroy the church, from executions during the early Roman Empire to the attacks that Christian missionaries face today. The church has endured some of the greatest persecutions known to humanity, yet, by God's grace and guidance, she has always emerged from the ashes as a victor. In keeping with Jesus' promise, *"the gates of Hades"* have not overcome the church—nor will they ever.

According to Scripture, the church is the Lord's "bride." He seeks after us, just as a man woos the woman he loves, and He anticipates the day when He will be fully united with His bride.

> *Now I saw a new heaven and a new earth, for the first heaven and the first earth had passed away. Also there was no more sea. Then I, John, saw the holy city, New Jerusalem, coming down out of heaven from God, prepared as a bride adorned for her husband. And I heard a loud voice from heaven saying, "Behold, the tabernacle of God is with men, and He will dwell with them, and they shall be His people. God Himself will be with them and be their God.* (Revelation 21:1–3)

The Lord is not going to let anything get in the way of that great wedding. He loves His bride and will continue to protect her as He has for so many years already.

## Hitting Close to Home: Your Congregation's Foundation

So, we've already established that the church—or God's people worldwide and throughout all time—is unshakable. Just like the Rock upon which she is built, the church is not going anywhere.

Knowing this to be true, we as Christians should daily strive to demonstrate in our lives the solidity of our Foundation. But how? How can I, as just one Christian in a world of billions of people, proclaim the steadfastness of my God? One way is by having a life that is solid, and I pray that this book has served, and will continue to serve, as a useful tool in your pursuit for personal solidity.

We can proclaim the steadfastness of our Lord in another way, as well, and that is through the church. If you are a Christian, you are part of God's church. As we've discussed, that church is rock-solid and able to stand the test of time.

How well does your local congregation pass this test? Is the group of believers that you regularly meet with solid? Is it built upon a strong foundation? If not, it will be sending mixed messages to those around you, for such a congregation fails to proclaim the truth that God's bride will be strong and standing in the end.

## A Good Solid Start

While teaching at Oral Roberts University's Mabee Center, author and pastor Dr. Myles Munroe related a story about a time he was invited to preach at a certain congregation. This church, less than one year old at the time, had experienced unprecedented growth in members nearly overnight. Dr. Munroe decided to approach the speaking assignment with caution and eventually declined the invitation, concluding that such a church might not be structured around the long-term goals and solid foundations which are crucial for any ministry of the Lord.

Of course, Dr. Munroe couldn't ignore the amazing church growth found early in the book of Acts. Three thousand souls were added to the church in a single day, the day of Pentecost, and five thousand more joined the church just a few days later. Dr. Munroe admitted that the sovereign hand of God could yield amazing results in the life of any ministry that was willing and ready to accept the high level of responsibility that inevitably comes with such growth.

But Dr. Munroe was suspicious of this particular church. After careful thought and prayer, he concluded that it had grown not through sound, responsible teaching of God's Word but rather through the use of gimmicks.

How a church begins is important because it paves the way for the ministry's growth and long-term health. For example, if a church initially lures people into attending by regularly hosting celebrity preachers, that church will have difficulty further down the road. Keeping people involved with the church would demand a steady stream of celebrities, and there certainly is not an unlimited supply of special guest speakers. Besides this difficulty, no church's growth should be based on who is behind the pulpit since Christ is the Rock upon which we should be building.

Similarly, if a church's primary emphasis is on hosting musicals, concerts, and special performances by well-known gospel artists, it will always need events like this to sustain the crowds and keep the people coming back. While music can play an important part in every worship service, it should never serve as a substitute for Scripture. I've noticed in churches where the primary emphasis is on music that the people are often left with a shallow understanding of God's Word. Because they have been trained to respond to music, which only requires a short attention span, they struggle when it comes time to receive teaching from God's Word.

## Staying Solid Until the End

In my years of ministry, I have seen many churches come and go. Those that remain have one thing in common: their solid foundation. Jesus has already built His church on a solid Foundation, and He desires every local congregation in His church to set itself upon solid foundations.

A church may look as if it is on the move for God and yet still not have enough foundation to last over time. Starting a church is relatively easy, but sustaining and leading it forward demands much greater responsibility and commitment. Anyone can start a church, but not everyone can lead a ministry that will last.

Sometimes a God-ordained ministry will be called on to survive lies, false allegations, schisms, and betrayals. How can a church continue growing when Satan has unleashed such a spirit of division? Only those churches that have built upon solid foundations from the start can survive storms like these.

## Sugar on Top?

What about those churches that have spent months, years, or even decades building on improper foundations. What are their options?

Let me answer you by posing a question of my own: Suppose you were baking a cake and realized halfway through the baking process that you had forgotten to add the sugar to the batter. What would you do? Would you let the cake keep baking, hoping it would turn out okay in the end by some great miracle? Would you wait until it was done baking and then sprinkle the required amount of sugar on top of the cooked cake? Neither of these solutions is reasonable. The only thing to do is start over and do it again—only right this time.

Just as you cannot pour sugar on top of an already baked cake and expect it to turn out okay, you cannot slap foundational principles on top of an improperly established ministry. You simply have to start from scratch, taking time to rethink, rework, and restructure the ministry according to God's principles. Although this may seem like a difficult task, it will not only save you time and effort in the long run but also help avert the crisis of collapse that can come to any structure built without a solid foundation.

# Chapter Nineteen
# Crumbling from Within: The Threat of Deadly Divisions

As we discussed earlier, one of the biggest threats that homeowners face is the possibility of cracks in the foundation. Certain cracks are bound to appear over time as the house shifts and settles into place, but deep, unexpected cracks are cause for concern. Water might seep through such cracks, eventually causing more foundational instability and the additional problem of moisture or water damage. Left untended, even the tiniest crack could ultimately mean the demise of an entire building's structural soundness.

## A Lesson from Our Lord

In a heated discussion with the Pharisees, Jesus taught an important lesson about division and the results it can have on an institution. Here's the scene: Jesus had just healed a man who was demon-possessed, blind, and mute. While everyone in the crowd started wondering if Jesus was the promised Messiah, the Pharisees accused Jesus of being anything but the promised Savior: *"Now when the Pharisees heard it they said, 'This fellow does not cast out demons except by Beelzebub, the ruler of the demons'"* (Matthew 12:24).

Beelzebub, the Philistine god of flies, is a name that has been attributed to the devil. In other words, the Pharisees accused Jesus of casting out demons by the power of Satan himself. The charges were so illogical that Jesus had no problem discrediting the Pharisees' accusations. He began asking them questions, and these questions quickly revealed the Pharisees' gross ignorance. On a side note, this method of questioning is a good habit to adopt. When you are falsely accused, don't try to defend yourself by arguing your case. Just begin asking questions of your accusers instead, allowing the burden of defense to lay on your opponent, not on yourself.

Think about how foolish these Pharisees must have looked before the crowd. Remember that the Pharisees were not merely religious zealots. They represented the finest religious scholars of that time! These men were very learned, yet their accusations were irrational and pointless, as Jesus was quick to point out.

> *But Jesus knew their thoughts, and said to them: "Every kingdom divided against itself is brought to desolation, and every city or house divided against itself will not stand. If Satan casts out Satan, he is divided against himself. How then will his kingdom stand? And if I cast out demons by Beelzebub, by whom do your sons cast them out? Therefore they shall be your judges."* (Matthew 12:25–27)

The man Jesus healed had been possessed by a demon, and Jesus wondered aloud why the devil would want to give power to Jesus to cast out his own spirit. This would have been senseless. Satan knew that he was at a disadvantage because Jesus ultimately had all power. Why would he want to empower the Lord to destroy him even further? Plain and simple, he wouldn't. The Pharisees' accusations just didn't hold water.

## Kingdoms Divided

We can glean an important lesson about organizational and institutional strength from Jesus' response to the Pharisees here. Any institution—whether it be a nation, a church, a business, a marriage, or a family—will eventually crumble if it is divided against itself: *"Every kingdom divided against itself is brought to desolation, and every city or house divided against itself will not stand"* (Matthew 12:25).

> Any institution—a church, nation, or family—will eventually crumble if it is divided against itself.

History is filled with examples of this principle. For instance, consider the Civil War that was fought on American soil. In this war, the Union and the Confederacy battled over several key issues, primarily the issues of slavery, economics, and state rights. This war, in which a once united nation divided in two, was costly, since many lives were lost and properties were destroyed.

While much good came from this war in the end—freedom for more than four million slaves and for future generations of African-Americans—no one can deny that the Civil War was costly. It divided us as a nation, and, as Jesus taught, a kingdom divided against itself cannot stand. By the grace of God, our country *did* pull through in one piece, but this is truly incredible and very rare. Much more common are situations like that of Rwanda.

The people of Rwanda have been at war for hundreds of years over issues of ethnic rights. During the mid-'90s, this ethnic strife came to a head, and the ensuing war dominated the news. Much blood was shed, and the Rwandan government and economy continued to weaken. Now, that country is again threatened—this time by the rise of the AIDS virus. Still, ethnic divisions within the country prevent the people from dealing effectively with these crises as a united people. Division in this nation has paved the way for more destruction and disaster.

# The Enemy Delights in Division

The enemy's method for getting a foothold in any situation is to first cause division and disagreement, for he, too, realizes the truth of Jesus' statement that *"every kingdom divided against itself is brought to desolation."* As much as he can, Satan wants to bring division and disagreement into the church.

Because of this, we must keep our eyes peeled for division. We should never encourage the development of division but instead fight against it. When we recognize division and disagreement within an institution that we're part of, we should take steps to reduce or even resolve that disagreement as quickly as possible: *"Therefore if you bring your gift to the altar, and there remember that your brother has something against you, leave your gift there before the altar, and go your way. First be reconciled to your brother, and then come and offer your gift"* (Matthew 5:23–24).

Please don't misunderstand me. I'm not saying that life can be perfect, conflict-free, and divisionless. There are bound to be disagreements and we should expect them. Not to do so would only be fooling ourselves. But through them all, we must come back to the basics: the glory of Christ and the furtherance of His Kingdom. Without these ends in mind, we will undoubtedly find ourselves in head-butting that may ultimately prove impossible to resolve. When the glory of the Lord and the forward march of His kingdom are our key concerns, however, we will have vision and wisdom enough to fight for those things that are essential and abandon those things that are not.

# Conclusion

Laying a foundation is not simple work. It takes time, patience, foresight, and a lot of sweat. When a builder starts putting down his foundation, he doesn't expect it to be a quick, easy, and immediately rewarding endeavor. He knows that the process may take awhile. He prepares himself for heavy lifting, tiresome digging, and many long hours in the mud. And he accepts the fact that he might not taste the fruits of his labor until several days, weeks, or even months down the road.

You see, laying a foundation is unlike any other house-building task. When it comes to other duties—like painting the walls, carpeting the floors, shingling the roof, or installing the windows—a person can see and appreciate the results right away. Most people like doing jobs like this because it gives them a sense of accomplishment. When they finish the task, they can sit back, look at it, and appreciate a job well done. A foundation, however, doesn't bring a quick sense of satisfaction. It is not until much later, when the rest of the house is actually resting on and relying upon that painstakingly laid foundation, that a builder can appreciate the time and effort he spent putting it in.

Quite frankly, foundations don't get the appreciation they deserve, either. Foundations are mostly underground. Most people rarely see them or even know that they're there! This is quite different from any other part of the house. For instance, imagine if a builder were to ask someone if he wanted a roof on his house or not. Can you imagine the looks that builder would get! "Are you crazy?" the customer might say. "Of course I want a roof!" Ask the same person if he wanted a foundation, however, and the response might not be nearly as animated. "The foundation?" he would ask. "That's down there with the basement and stuff, right? Well, I guess I'll need one of those....Sure, put one in."

While everyone understands the significance of roofs, few understand the imperativeness of foundations. Without a foundation, a house cannot stand. Since the foundation is seldom seen, however, few people stop to think about this.

Foundations in our own lives are much the same way. They take time. They take a lot of hard work. They don't seem important until later on when we see how much of our current tasks actually rely on the foundation we have already laid. And they often don't get the appreciation that they deserve.

Think about Noah and the ark. God had a plan for saving Noah and his family from the Flood, but it didn't just happen overnight. It took planning and the long process of building an ark.

*And God said to Noah, "The end of all flesh has come before Me, for the earth is filled with violence through them; and behold, I will destroy them with the earth. Make yourself an ark of gopherwood; make rooms in the ark, and cover it inside and outside with pitch. And this is how you shall make it: The length of the ark shall be three hundred cubits, its width fifty cubits, and its height thirty cubits. You shall make a window for the ark, and you shall finish it to a cubit from above; and set the door of the ark in its side. You shall make it with lower, second, and third decks. And behold, I Myself am bringing floodwaters on the earth, to destroy from under heaven all flesh in which is the breath of life; everything that is on the earth shall die. But I will establish My covenant with you; and you shall go into the ark; you, your sons, your wife, and your sons' wives with you."* (Genesis 6:13–18)

I'm sure Noah would have liked a much quicker, easier solution. "God, couldn't You just put me on top of a really, really, really tall mountain made especially for this purpose?" he might have asked. Through this experience, however, Noah learned an important truth that we all need to learn: God's methods are very different from and far superior to our methods. *"For My thoughts are not your thoughts, nor are your ways My ways....For as the heavens are higher than the earth, so are My ways higher than your ways, and My thoughts than your thoughts"* (Isaiah 55:8–9).

You see, our Lord is a master builder. As Creator of the universe, He holds skills that the greatest of architects and builders can never hope to attain. And one thing He never overlooks when He's building is the necessity of foundations. He doesn't impatiently jump ahead to end results; instead, He first lays the groundwork required to attain those end results, and He expects no less from His children. For Noah, this meant spending time carefully constructing an ark. For Moses, this meant living many years as an Egyptian so He would have an "in" with Pharaoh when it came time to ask permission for the Hebrews to leave. With Abraham, this meant many childless years of learning how to trust God before moving even a step closer to the offspring promised to be *"as many as the stars of the sky in multitude; innumerable as the sand which is by the seashore"* (Hebrews 11:12). With Jesus, this meant thirty years of preparation before His years of public ministry even started: *"Now Jesus Himself began His ministry at about thirty years of age"* (Luke 3:23).

I think you'll agree that our Lord is very interested in foundations. Man would love to hit the spiritual lottery—to wake up one morning and have a perfect faith, a perfect ministry, a perfect prayer life. Or, in the social realm, man would love to roll that pair of sixes, securing him a lifetime of stress-free and fulfilling friendships. And, in the work world, wouldn't it be great to make a single move that would ensure success forever?

But God doesn't work this way. He calls on His children to invest, just as He has invested, in laying foundations. Whatever He calls you to—whether it be raising your children at home or raising walls for the new four-thousand-seat sanctuary of your church—take time to lay a solid foundation. Even more importantly, make sure every step of the way that the Lord is your ultimate Foundation, the solid Rock upon which every other foundation is laid.

But He is not just your Foundation; He is the Master Architect, as well. He is the Source of everything that is true, good, solid, and stable in your life. He deserves all the glory and all the praise. Please make sure He gets it. It is only then that your life will be in line with the Master's perfect plan.

# About the Author
# Dr. LeRoy Bailey Jr.

D r. LeRoy Bailey Jr. is the senior pastor and chief executive officer for The First Cathedral, in Bloomfield, Connecticut, a congregation that has grown under Dr. Bailey's leadership from a few hundred members in 1971 to more than ten thousand today. He is a gifted teacher, preacher, and counselor, whose love for the Lord has lead him to equip believers for service. First Cathedral has mission outreaches in Africa, Haiti, and St. Lucia, as well as its own elementary school and accredited college.

Dr. Bailey was born and raised in Memphis, Tennessee. He received a B.A. in sociology from American Baptist College in Nashville, Tennessee; a Masters of Divinity from Howard University in Washington, D.C.; an Honorary Doctor of Divinity from Tennessee Baptist School of Religion in Memphis; a Doctor of Ministry from Hartford Seminary in Hartford, Connecticut; and an Honorary Doctorate from Biblical Life College and Seminary in Marshville, Missouri.

Dr. Bailey is the presiding bishop of an organization known as the Churches Covered and Connected in Covenant

(CCCC). He is also a member of the General Council of Churches United Global in Anaheim, California, a founder of Pastors in Covenant (a mentoring program for pastors across the United States), president of the Chaplaincy Corp for the Hartford Police Department, a board member for the Hospice Association, and a member of Vision New England. Dr. Bailey has also served as chairman of the Luis Palau Crusade, 2001.

For more than twenty-five years, Dr. Bailey has been married to Reathie Bailey. They have three children: Riva Nelva Bailey, a graduate of Johnson C. Smith College and an elementary school teacher at the First Academy in Bloomfield; LeRoy Bailey III, a graduate of the University of Hartford in Hartford, Connecticut, and the coordinator of audio-visual ministry at The First Cathedral; and Michael David Bailey, a student at Gordon College in Wenham, Massachusetts.

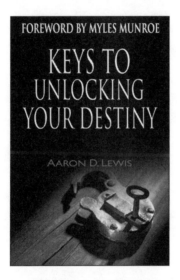

# ANOTHER POWERFUL **B**OOK
## from Whitaker House

DR. MYLES MUNROE

BEST-SELLING AUTHOR

UNDERSTANDING THE PURPOSE AND POWER OF

# PRAYER

EARTHLY LICENSE FOR HEAVENLY INTERFERENCE

### Understanding the Purpose and Power of Prayer
*Dr. Myles Munroe*

All that God is—and all that God has—may be received through prayer. Everything you need to fulfill your purpose on earth is available to you through prayer. The biblically-based, time-tested principles presented by Dr. Myles Munroe will ignite and transform the way you pray. Be prepared to enter into a new dimension of faith, a deeper revelation of God's love, and a renewed understanding that your prayers can truly move the hand of God.

ISBN: 0-88368-442-X • Trade • 240 pages

# OTHER POWERFUL *B*OOKS
## from Whitaker House

### Understanding the Purpose and Power of Men
#### Dr. Myles Munroe

Today, the world is sending out conflicting signals about what it means to be a man. Many men are questioning who they are and what roles they fulfill in life—as a male, a husband, and a father. Best-selling author Myles Munroe examines cultural attitudes toward men and discusses the purpose God has given them. Discover the destiny and potential of the man as he was meant to be.

ISBN: 0-88368-725-9
Trade   224 pages

### Understanding the Purpose and Power of Woman
#### Dr. Myles Munroe

To live successfully in the world, women need to know what role they play. They need a new awareness of who they are, and new skills to meet today's challenges. Myles Munroe helps women to discover who they are. Whether you are a woman or a man, married or single, this book will help you to understand the woman as she was meant to be.

ISBN: 0-88368-671-6
Trade   208 pages

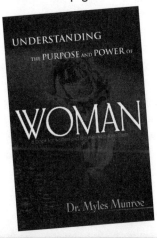

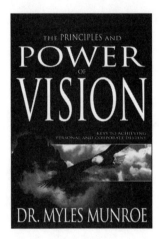